SENGAI
The Zen Master

SENGAI
The Zen Master

by

DAISETZ T. SUZUKI

with editorial and prefatory notes by
Eva van Hoboken, Sazo Idemitsu
Basil Gray and Herbert Read

FABER AND FABER
London

First published in 1971
by Faber and Faber Limited
3 Queen Square London WC 1
Printed in Great Britain by
R. MacLehose & Co. Ltd
The University Press, Glasgow
All rights reserved

ISBN 0 571 08444 3

CONTENTS

v

ILLUSTRATIONS

INK DRAWINGS AND CALLIGRAPHIES
related to Sengai's life at the temples

INK DRAWINGS AND CALLIGRAPHIES

EDITOR'S NOTE

Asaying of Dr. Daisetz Suzuki was that one has not truly understood the doctrine of Zen until one has forgotten it. He made a life-long study of Zen Buddhism, following in this the way taken by the great Japanese Zen master Sengai, abbot of the Shōfukuji, the oldest Zen temple in Japan. During his long life Dr. Suzuki was able to promote the study of Zen in the West as well as in the East, and his scholarship became world-famous, but, like Sengai, he never lost sight of the true purpose of his studies: to teach the state of inner freedom, or enlightenment. For this reason his texts and comments on Sengai's drawings and sayings enable Sengai's own communication to reach the modern reader. Suzuki's wisdom and humour are from the same inner source as Sengai's: the lightheartedness of the drawings and words on the sorrows and joys of daily life express also the transcendental wisdom of Zen.

In an interview with a Japanese scholar, towards the end of his life, Dr. Suzuki mentioned the possibility that, after being brought from China to Japan, and nourished and developed there for a thousand years, Zen may die out in Japan, and it may now be for the West to preserve the doctrine. If it is not truly understood there, and fails to take firm root, knowledge of it may disappear, although the essence of Zen is eternal.

Dr. Suzuki considered his explanatory notes and texts on Sengai's scrolls as the summing-up of his own work. He wrote them in English, and his last wish was that this book, the last that he completed in his ninety-five years of life, should be published in the West, and his original text has not been changed. The editor must express her gratitude to all the people who helped in the fulfilment of this wish: notably Mr. Sazo Idemitsu, the owner of the precious scrolls; the late Sir Herbert Read, pioneer writer on modern art; Mr. Basil Gray, until recently Keeper of Oriental Antiquities in the British Museum; Professor Shōkin Furuta, Director at the Pine Hill Library in Kamakura; Mr. Richard de la Mare of Faber and Faber, the publisher, who is also a connoisseur of Japanese Ceramics; Mr. Brian Rooney, also of Faber and Faber, who has looked after the book's production; also to Mr. Christmas Humphreys, President of the Buddhist Society, and to the Rev. Jikai Murakami, Abbot of Kinkakuji, the Golden Pavilion, London, Kyoto, for their moral support.

Ascona, February 1970   EVA VAN HOBOKEN

SENGAI'S DRAWINGS AND MYSELF

Sengai in his later years lived in Hakata (Fukuoka), which happens to be my native place, where he left a number of his Zen drawings. One day, when I was about nineteen years old, I accompanied my father on one of his visits to art dealers in the town and I saw Sengai's drawings for the first time. Then and there, I was captivated by his work and begged my father to buy one for me. This was No. 113 in this book depicting Hotei (Pu-tai, one of the Seven Gods of Good Luck). In those days, when I had just started my own business, not very long after leaving school, the drawings of Sengai were moderate in price and within my means. So after business trips, I usually found that some of Sengai's drawings had been brought in by art dealers during my absence, and it was a great pleasure for me to look at them. When none had been brought in I felt as if something important was missing. This went on for about sixty years, and resulted in my present large collection.

But, although I collected Sengai's drawings, I did not pay much attention to who or what he was for about forty years. I knew him simply as a witty, unconventional and interesting monk. It was quite a long time before I happened to learn that he was one of the famous masters in the history of Zen known by the name of Entsu-Zenji. Face to face with his drawings, day in, day out, however, I cannot deny that unconsciously I was greatly influenced and inspired by his works. Indeed, I owe much to Sengai-san for my happy life.

It is now sixteen years since I started reproducing Sengai's drawings on my Company's calendars, which have been received very favourably abroad as well as in Japan, with requests for them increasing every year till some eight hundred thousand copies were printed for distribution in 1970. I believe that these Sengai calendars contribute much to the happy and harmonious life of those who received them, and I intend to continue to use them as long as my collection permits.

In April and May, 1956, Japanese Zen drawings were exhibited at the Japan Cultural Festival in Oakland, Calif., U.S.A., an exhibition for which I loaned some twenty-two of Sengai's works. I had a simple catalogue prepared in English for this occasion with the hope that it might assist visitors to the exhibition to understand the drawings. At that time, Dr. Daisetz T. Suzuki happened to be in New York and, after seeing the catalogue, he wrote to me, saying that he felt as if he were writing to a friend of very, very long standing, tied as it were, by the common love of Sengai's drawings. This marked the start of my relationship with Suzuki-sensei.

It may be superfluous for me to tell about Suzuki-sensei. Suffice it to say that a poetess, Mrs. Eva van Hoboken, who put herself under his guidance, became, after two years, a prime mover for the exhibitions of Sengai's works held afterwards in fourteen important Museums and Art Galleries in Europe between the years 1961 and 1964. Their success was immense and remarkable for its continuance over such a long period. These successes in Europe, which created quite a sensation in certain quarters, led to another exhibition in New Zealand, in Spring, 1966, and now plans are afoot for putting on others in Australia, in the U.S.A., and in the U.S.S.R. Thus I have become more and more convinced that the virtues of Sengai's drawings are unfathomably great.

In 1961, I asked Suzuki-sensei to come and spend the summer at my villa in Karuizawa, and after that he came every summer to study. It was, as I remember, during the summer of 1963, that our talks drifted in some way or other to the idea of publishing a book in English on Sengai's works. And once the idea came into my head, I became eager with the desire for its realization. Thus Suzuki-sensei started to work on it, saying that he would have to live five years more in order to complete what he planned to do. I used to find him hard at work with admirable enthusiasm making use of every moment of leisure from his busy life in spite of being already over ninety years old. Finally, after much thought and elaboration over three years, he finished the first series of his manuscripts covering 127 works. Then, on the morning of July 12, 1966, when about to leave for Karuizawa, to give the final touch to his writings at my villa, he suddenly succumbed to the illness from which he never recovered.

In this sudden manner, the great follower and scholar of Zen fell. For a moment I looked back upon and meditated over the warm guidance I was given based on his firm belief. Of course I was filled with deep grief. But he left a priceless legacy in the form of his MSS on Sengai which I felt duty bound to publish in a

fine book as a reminder of his great virtue and for the benefit of people everywhere. It is, therefore, my earnest desire that, through the painstaking commen-
taries of Dr. Suzuki, more and more people will appreciate the virtue of Sengai's
Zen and works. And so, if this book serves as a guide for all human beings to
walk on the path that leads eventually to world peace and harmony, I shall indeed
be a very happy man.

Tokyo, 1970   SAZO IDEMITSU

SENGAI AND HIS PREDECESSORS

Sengai, we are told, was 'not a professional artist'; but this does not mean that he differed essentially from many other priest artists. He was certainly in close touch with the Zen *suiboku* ink technique, which had been constantly renewed in Japan by the arrival of Chinese refugee priests, especially under the Mongol and Manchu rule. In the eighteenth century the Zen priestly tradition of vigorous dissent was linked in its stress on sincerity and spontaneity with the scholarly, *Bunjinga* (Chinese: Wên jên hua) contempt for the academic or finished work of the professional painter. It is this positive tradition of 'ink-play' into which Sengai so joyously entered. It is worth recalling that he grew up just when Yosa Buson (1716–83), the greatest exponent of this Nanga or Chinese tradition, was entering on his final phase, in which in the 1770's he united his skill as a Haiku poet with his mastery of the brush to produce *haiga*, a popular and unbuttoned style of linked aphoristic poem and sketch. The two may never have met, but it must be assumed that Sengai was acquainted with Buson's late work. For it was not until he was forty that Sengai withdrew to Hakata in Kyûshû, and while living under his master Gessen Zenji at Nagata from 1770 to 1783, he would have been in contact with the most vital movement of the period in Zen circles, led by Ike no Taiga (1723–1776) and Yosa Buson.

The intimate association of *haiku* poem and illustration in Sengai's work derives from this movement. The tradition among Zen priests was of mastery of the art of calligraphy and of its parallel esteem with the art of painting, with which of course it was intimately linked by technical identity of the medium. This tradition was particularly strong in Kyûshû, to which Sengai went when migrating to Shôfukuji, where he was abbot until 1811. It was with the southern island of Kyûshû that Chinese influence has always been most direct because of its proximity to the coasts of China and Korea. Sengai was therefore the inheritor of a tradition of brushwork such as we have never enjoyed in the West: and his writing was prized for just the qualities which had been admired for centuries past. His admiration for the greatest of the *haiku* poets, Bashô (1644–94) is specifically seen in one of the calligraphies exhibited in London in 1962, which consists of his name only; and more explicitly in the triptych (no. 110), 'Bashô and the Frog', which is no more than a gloss on a famous *haiku* poem of Bashô. It is normal to find a deeper appreciation of the work of an artist when it is seen in the context of its time and place, and there is no exception with Sengai, who is not to be thought of as some isolated protester, but as part of a perennial tradition of protest against worldliness in the Zen exponents of detachment.

No doubt it is this vigorous dissent which appeals most to us in the 1970's. Sengai was the enemy of every form of 'establishment', but he could not have made so effective a protest if he had not been equipped with the weapons of the *haiku* poem, the brush tradition of painting and calligraphy and the Zen passion for the enlightenment of humour.

August 1970   BASIL GRAY

PREFACE

Arepresentative collection of Sengai's work was shown in the principal
museums and art galleries of Europe in 1961–64. As a result the name
of this great Japanese artist became familiar to thousands of people,
and this has led to a demand for some permanent record of the exhibition. The catalogue has been thoroughly revised, and one of the last tasks of
Dr. Suzuki, before he died at the age of ninety-five, was to complete the essay
on Sengai which introduces this volume. Daisetz Suzuki, one of the great sages
of our time, would describe himself as a disciple of Sengai, and no one else
could write about the artist with such deep sympathy and understanding. But he
would have been the first to admit that Sengai is not for the specialist: he is a
very human, even a popular artist, and deserves to become known to all lovers of
art. This has now been made possible by the generosity of Mr. Sazo Idemitsu,
parts of whose collection of Sengai's work is presented in this volume.

It is difficult to find a European parallel for Sengai. The lowliness of his subject-
matter and the fluidity of his line may remind us of some of Daumier's drawings
or etchings; his satirical point of view and the swiftness of his notations sometimes
suggests the *Caprichos* of Goya. But neither of these great artists has the variety
of Sengai — neither could have conceived, to make a small choice, *Sengai's Poem
on Himself* (I), or *The Universe* (1), or *The Plum-Blossoms* (80), or *The Bullfinch*
(107), or *The Floating Gourd* (115), or *The Meditating Frog* (40). Sengai is various
and he is unique. One is tempted to call him a transcendental humorist, but one
must then allow for his lyricism, for his love of nature, and for his wholly serious
paintings (like the *Amida Butsu* (2)). But it is through his wit and humour that he
expresses his deepest purpose, which is not so much to amuse us, as to enlighten
us by means of amusement. Musing, amusing — the words have a close connection
in English, and might perhaps be used to indicate the significance of Sengai's art.

'Musing' implies ironic or reflective detachment (literally 'standing with muzzle in the air'), that standing aloof from the grave and solemn business of life which Dr. Suzuki gives as the characteristic feature of Zen. Amusement is the reaction of the free heart to the sorry spectacle of the world. But the heart that is free is also engaged, and Sengai's amusement, as expressed in his drawings, is a 'direct relation'. This is the phrase used by a Western philosopher to describe the relation of the 'I' to the 'Thou' and to the 'It'. This philosopher, Martin Buber, has a few words which perfectly describe Sengai's attitude to the things and people he saw and recorded:

'Believe in the simple magic of life, in service in the universe, and the meaning of that waiting, that alertness, that ''craning of the neck'' in creatures, will dawn upon you. Every word would falsify; but look! round about you beings live their life, and to whatever point you turn you come upon being.'

It is 'being' in this sense that Sengai records so swiftly, so spontaneously, without falsification. Persons and things, the self and nature, good and evil, all related and interrelated, synchronous and constellated. Only judgement seems alien — or as Sengai himself put it:

> Just because (we are)
> In the midst of good and evil.
> This cool evening breeze!

A deeply sympathetic character, a brilliant calligrapher, a profound mystic, Sengai comes to Europe to educate us, to lead us out of confusion, to teach us the simple magic of life.

HERBERT READ

INTRODUCTION TO SENGAI
by Daisetz T. Suzuki

INTRODUCTION TO SENGAI

Sengai, the author of all these ink-drawings and calligraphies, was not a professional artist, nor was he a critic of human life bent on satirically and humorously depicting it. He was first and last a Zen monk and teacher who loved humanity, always desiring to promote peace and happiness on earth. He took also a transcendental view of things that are relative and limited. One eye was turned deeply inward, while the other looked out with concern to catch the fleeting shadows of our earthly life. He sympathized with the people around him and shared their sufferings, but he never lost himself in them. There was some strength in him which gave him enough room for witticism and humour.

In fact, there is something in Zen itself that makes Zen people laugh at one another, and each singly within himself. When they avow that Zen is not dependent on verbalism they are quite in earnest, and no doubt they are right. But actually they cannot keep their mouths closed. If they do they cannot make themselves intelligible to others or even to themselves. They have somehow to speak out, they have to break their silence. Indeed the silence itself is a negation, and a negation negates something; and this something speaks out of the midst of the negation. That is to say, the silence of Vimalakīrti ends in contradicting itself. Hence its great eloquence. We efface ourselves in spite of ourselves, which is laughable. This is the way the Zen masters assert and deny at the same time. Zen is thus always the subject of mutual ridiculing among its adherents. Not just ridiculing, it frequently bursts out in a loud cry or a roaring exclamation, and when pedagogy is involved, it leads even to a striking or a kicking. Zen always wishes to keep itself as close as possible to Reality, so that it will never wander out into the world of concepts or symbols.

To illustrate this point, a few examples from annals of Zen are given as follows:

(1) Bodhidharma, legendarily regarded as the first patriarch of Chinese Zen, who came to China in circa 520, is recorded as having had an interview with the Emperor Wu of the Liang dynasty in Southern China. The first question the Emperor asked was:

'What is the primary truth of the Holy Teaching?'

Bodhidharma answered, 'Vastly empty and nothing holy.'

Engo (Yüan-wu, 1062–1135), the compiler of the Blue Cliff Collection, comments as follows, first on the Truth of the Holy Teaching: 'What a donkey-post this is!' Then on Bodhidharma himself: 'Oh, this fellow who talks nonsense!'

The reader may wonder how a Buddhist could make such a derogatory remark about the first reality on which his teaching is based. As to Bodhidharma himself, what an outrageous evaluation! But Engo does not stop with this. When it comes to Bodhidharma's answer 'Vastly empty and nothing holy', Engo bluntly gives this: 'I thought it might be wonderfully extraordinary [but how commonplace!]' While Bodhidharma's answer itself is somewhat disappointing or even arrogant from the conventional point of view, how could a follower of the school of Bodhidharma insult his leader's statement by designating it as commonplace and nothing wonderful?

Generally speaking, Zen masters are no more respecters of personality than of conceptualism. Their eye is fixed on something beyond all forms of limitation and definability, and they would criticise others from this higher attitude of their own. When thus the Emperor further asked Bodhidharma, 'Who are you then [who is regarded as a holy transmitter of Buddha's doctrine]?' Bodhidharma unceremoniously replied, 'I do not know.' On this, Engo comments, 'Tut! Again, not worth a penny!' This is not necessarily Engo's sarcasm. Inasmuch as he is bent on warning people not to be enticed by words or concepts, he is, we must admit, justified in using such strong caustic language. We are also to remember that Bodhidharma here has nothing to do with agnosticism.

(2) There is a well-reported episode which happened to one of Rinzai's disciples. Jō the Elder once approached Rinzai (Lin-chi, d. 866) and asked, 'What is the essence of Buddha's teaching?' Rinzai, coming down from his chair, approached the monk and, taking hold of his chest, slapped his face and let him go. Jō did not know what this meant and stood still, dumbfounded. The attendant

monk suggested, 'Why don't you bow to the master?' While trying to bow as told, Jō the Elder came upon a great awakening.

Engo comments on the question, 'What is the essence of Buddha's teaching?' thus: 'What a dotard to ask such [a time-worn] question!' On Rinzai's treatment of the monk, Engo remarks, 'How grandmotherly!' This is quite appropriate, but how about Engo's comments on the question which concerns all earnest Buddhists? Engo makes another slanderous statement on Jō's 'great awakening': 'What did he see here?' — as if to say 'there is after all nothing to see. What a fuss!' 'One error leads to another', Engo goes on to say, as if Jō's first question was a great error which logically continues to his final one known as 'great awakening'. All in all, Engo's appraisal of this episode between Rinzai and his pupil Jō the Elder is, apparently, much ado about nothing.

(3) Gutei Oshō (Chü-chih), who probably flourished in the latter part of the ninth century, raised one of his fingers as the only answer to whatever question was presented to him. Chōkei (Ch'ang-ch'ing, 855–932), one of his contemporaries, remarked, 'How sumptuous the feast, it fails to tempt the one whose stomach is already filled.'

When Gutei was about to depart, he told his disciples, 'Since I attained to the understanding of Tenryū's (T'ien-lung) "one finger" I have never been able to exhaust its meaning all my life. Do you wish to know what it is?' So saying, he raised one finger and passed away in the manner a spirit would shed its outer garment. Later Meishō Dokuganryū asked Kokutai Shin, 'I understand that Gutei came to the meaning of one finger by means of a three-line dhārani. Pray tell me what this three-line dhārani is.' Shin raised his finger, which made Meishō's eye open.

This mysterious 'one finger' of Gutei, Zen would declare, is not a symbol for anything, it is the reality itself, it is the 'one hair' of a lion on the top of which the Kegon tells us are seen millions and millions of lions dancing. It is really 'the sumptuous dinner' displayed ungrudgingly before Chōkei on which however he would contemptuously remark, saying, 'The sumptuous feast fails to tempt me.'

Gensha (Hsüan-sha, 834–908), another contemporary, comments, 'If I saw him hold up his finger, I would have broken it by giving it a hard twist!' When Gutei's one finger is taken as a symbol or a concept it is worth nothing; it is only when it is really itself that it holds in it heaven and earth and the ten thousand things. This kind of finger can never be broken and thrown on the dunghill. Zen always tries to see in Gutei's the reality-finger and not a symbol-finger. Zen's apparently slighting, belittling, self-conceited attitude toward what is generally revered as holy or of deep significance is due to its eye always being on Reality itself and not on an empty concept. We must remember this. But as far as the appearance goes, these remarks by the masters are, to say the least, outrageous.

(4) Jōshū (Chao-chou, 778–897) was one of the most brilliant T'ang masters. He was asked by a disciple, 'All things return to One, and where does the One return?' Answered the master, 'When I was in Seijū (Ching-chou), I had a robe made which weighed seven kin (chin).'

Secchō (Hsüeh-tou, 980–1052) comments:

'Let all now be thrown away into the Western Lake:

The fine breeze — who is going to enjoy it to his heart's content?'

Engo interprets: 'To throw away means to throw away the robe weighing seven kin as well as the One to which all the ten thousand things return. Rid yourself of both, be thoroughly free from all possible forms of limitation and definability, and then you will find yourself behaving like a sail boat that follows the wind blowing over the Lake.'

The question of the One is of great philosophical significance and most religiously-minded people would approach it with a sense of reverence and awe. They would never think of treating the subject so indifferently, as if it were a matter of buying a robe or of throwing away a worn-out one into a lake and be enjoying a cool breeze on the summer evening. The Zen master's attitude, whatever its pedagogical motive, is essentially one of common sense, one may say.

All in all, Zen is something immeasurably drastic and unconventional in the world history of thought. As long as it keeps its eye on the Infinite, in fact even beyond the Infinite, so to speak, it naturally finds something unique and makes some, even many, Buddhists themselves denounce it as satanic or demoniac. This may be going too far, but the fact is that Zen always takes care to keep its followers within certain bounds until they are practically and morally trained to really behave in the way the Zen-man should.

Incidentally, to illustrate this, let me cite the following: Ōbaku Ki-un (Huang-po Hsi-yün, died some time 847–60), an older contemporary of Jōshū's, is a renowned master of the T'ang. In the monastery where Ōbaku was the leading monk, there was a novice of the imperial lineage who was later enthroned. The novice once seeing Ōbaku engaged in reciting the Sūtra asked him: 'I am told "not to seek [the truth] by means of the Buddha, nor by means of the Dharma, nor by means of the Sangha". If so, what do you seek by bowing to the Buddha?'

4

Answered Ōbaku, 'I do not seek by means of the Buddha, nor by means of the Dharma, nor by means of the Sangha. And I bow to the Buddha thus.'

'What is the use of bowing then?'

Ōbaku without saying anything struck the monk.

The monk protested, 'How rude you are!'

Ōbaku said, 'Where do you think you are? There is no room here to talk about rude or fine.'

This was followed by another blow.

3

From these considerations it is clear now, and natural I think, that the Zen master finds something comic in our earthly affairs including himself, and turns them all into subjects for laughter, though not at all with ill-will or with a derisive attitude. He is full of human love and at the same time there is what Meister Eckhart calls *Abgeschiedenheit* (*anabhiniveśa*, disinterest) in him. He is in it and yet not attached to it; he is living in the world as if not in it. The humorous spirit that pervades Sengai's pictures is the expression of his genuine humanism; nothing of cold self-alienating cynicism there!

Sengai is no doubt transcendental in his witticisms, but we must remember that he is also an immanentist. He is one of us, he lives in us, with us, and shares all our woes. This is his *karunā* (love). A good Zen monk is an embodiment of *mahāprajñā* (absolute wisdom) and of *mahākarunā* (absolute love). It is the first aspect that makes him a transcendentalist and it is the second aspect that makes him come down from his high position and become a great humanist. He cannot be a mere cynic. When Sengai was once referred to as a Zen monk who played with the brush to laugh at human infirmities, he retorted, 'No, I am not. Every stroke of my brush is the overflow of my inmost heart.' He did not like to see his work being turned into 'wrapping paper', as if his products were mere pastime nonsense.

I said before that Sengai was not a professional artist, and when he took up his brush and faced a sheet of paper in front of him, did he not feel something, though much more complicated, like a boy playing ball? As his creative artistic impulse dictated the movement of his brush did he not feel something of sportiveness inwardly?

Ryōkwan, Sengai's contemporary and friend, used to play a game called *temari* with his friends, generally a group of small girls. He enjoyed it immensely, as he watched the young hands busily moving over the bouncing ball, accompanied by simple songs. The girls have no idea of life objectively, they feel it simply inwardly and this is translated into arms and hands. As Ryōkwan watches he feels it himself. When a girl fails to catch the ball, Ryōkwan's turn comes and he takes it up and goes on with the same rhythmic motion of the body. It is likely that Ryōkwan's handling of the ball was not so deftly executed and the ball got out of his control after a few trials and set the whole company laughing. But this grown-up, mature man, with full knowledge of the world, was probably the heartiest laugher of them all. So with Sengai. He must have innerly gone through something of Ryōkwan's laughter.

Kierkegaard gives us an interesting dream he had while young.

'Something marvellous has happened to me. I was caught up into the seventh heaven. There sat all the gods in assembly. As a special grace there was accorded to me the privilege of making a wish. "Wilt thou," said Mercury, "wilt thou have youth, or beauty, or power, or long life, or the most beautiful maiden, or any other glorious thing among the many we have here in the treasure-chest? Then choose, but only one thing." For an instant I was irresolute, then I addressed the gods as follows: "Highly esteemed contemporaries, I choose one thing, that I may always have the laugh on my side." There was not a god that answered a word, but they all burst out laughing. Thereupon I concluded that my wish was granted, and I found that the gods knew how to express themselves with good taste; for it surely would have been inappropriate for them to answer seriously, "This is conceded to thee." ' (*Trans. by Walter Lowrie.*)

Not Kierkegaard's interpretation, but something which moved in the gods' subjectivity at the time of their hearty laughter. Did not something of this sort also enter, however unconsciously, into Sengai's movement of the brush?

4

Sengai occupied the position of abbot in the first Zen temple ever built in Japan, by Eisai (1141–1215) (Plate 27) who came back in 1191 from his second visit to China which had lasted six years. While in office Sengai must have been pretty busily engaged in the management of the temple. It was after his retirement, when he was sixty-one, that he spent his remaining twenty-four years free from worldly affairs. He then devoted his life to a full display of his artistic activity. He may not have been professionally trained in the technique of ink-drawing or painting, but his natural endowments as an artist of life and human nature were rich; the imagination we see in his work testifies to it. His humour overflows in his drawings, but they betray no ill temper; they are not at all ironic or sarcastic, but filled with a compassionate heart and with good will for all humanity and non-sentient beings alike.

In his Preface, Sir Herbert Read writes, 'One is tempted to call him a transcendental humorist'. This is very suggestive. Sengai's transcendentalism comes from his Zen, and his humorous playfulness too. When one sees directly into ultimate reality and can survey the world of relativities from this angle he feels a sense of detachment toward things around him; detachment because they are all seen as passing in time. When this contemplation is transferred into the inwardness of things it is the feeling of *myō*, or wonder. *Myō* (*miao* in Chinese) is a difficult term to translate. And this *myō* has an aspect of playfulness which is not merely amusement; it is accompanied with a sense of mystery or magic which is altogether entrancing.

I do not think theologians can ever laugh. They are too serious, too occupied in trying to identify themselves with the things of God, leaving no room for playfulness. For playfulness comes out of empty nothingness, and where there is something, this cannot take place. Zen comes out of absolute nothingness and knows how to be playful. In China, Sung masters such as Secchō, Engo, Daie (Tai-hui), and others did this in words, characteristic of the Chinese genius; in Japan Sengai and others did this with a brush on paper. A stick of bamboo about a foot long tipped with a tuft of sheep's hair produced Kanzan (Han-shan) and Jittoku (Shih-tê) (Plates 30, 39) in the midst of their enjoyment of 'the simple magic of life' as readily and merrily as men of the world drinking and dancing and singing under the cherry-blossoms (Plates 77, 83). The difference between these two types is that while the laughter of Kanzan and Jittoku is genuine, that of the merry-makers is spurious, forced and altogether superficial because of their not being able to penetrate into the source of being.

Laughter is the monopoly of human beings. Animals laugh seldom, the angels never. The devil laughs, but he is a mocker and is adept in the art of simulation and deception. Among human beings however only those have genuine laughter who have their abode in the kingdom of nothingness. Eckhart tells us in his

Sermons, 'God plays and laughs in good deeds' (Blakney, p. 143). But the question here is: what is meant by 'good deed'? What does Eckhart mean by 'good'? Most people may take the term in the moral sense and say that what God likes to see in us is our morally good behaviour, good standing against evil. My interpretation is different. 'Good' here means all that comes out of the pure heart of disinterest (or detachment, that is, *Abgeschiedenheit*), which is empty, with nothing in it, and in which 'my isness is God's isness', a complete identity of the two. Where there is a something left as among other somethings, no genuine laughter can come out. The good abides only where 'the simple magic of life' is actively enacted and felt inwardly. Eckhart states, 'God is free to do his will on his own level when my heart, being disinterested, is bent on neither this nor that', which is no other than 'the formless essence'. Laughter comes out of this essence of empty nothingness. Sengai tries to illustrate it in his drawings of Hotei (Plates 12, 14, 113, 118).

Let me quote here Eckhart's conversation with a beggar on 'good', which is illuminating in this connection.

Meister Eckhart spoke to a poor man.

'God give you good morning, brother!'

'The same to you, sir, but I have never yet had a bad one.'

'How is that, brother?'

'Because whatever God has sent me, I have borne gladly for his sake, considering myself unworthy of him. That is why I have never been sad or troubled.'

'Where did you first find God?'

'When I left all creatures, then I found God.'

'Where, then, did you leave him, brother?'

'In any clear, pure heart.' (*Meister Eckhart*, trans. by Blakney, pp. 251–2.)

The good of Eckhart's 'good morning' is not an ordinary good. It is the same good as the one which God is said to have uttered when he inspected the whole creation after everything was there as he had ordered. 'All is good!' This good has nothing to do with moral good, it is a kind of aesthetic good, the feeling we may have when we face 'the clear cool stream running through the middle of the reeds of good and evil' (No. 54). It is also the feeling that a man of empty nothingness may have had when he left all creatures. Eckhart's 'Good morning' as well as that of his beggar or poor man who has nothing of the created in 'his clear pure heart' of emptiness is the one who is referred to in the Confucian *Book of the Mean*: 'Let every day be a renewed one, let it for ever be a renewed one', which is continued creation.

8

This eternal good must have been Sengai's inwardness which created all his so-called 'playful' pictures. Sengai somewhere writes that his pictures do not follow any rules of convention, that they have their own laws which are really no-laws, just as Buddha says that his Dharma is no-Dharma. The no-Dharma is Eckhartian good, which is God's subjectivity, whereby the Biblical scribe was enabled to record this: 'God saw everything that he had made, and behold, it was very good' (Genesis, I. 31).

5

In the following I give three different occasions on which masters burst into laughter, in which each appreciates in his own way the goodness of reality. They will help us understand Sengai's laughter, expressed or implicit, in his humorous ink-drawings.

Kingyū (Chin-niu), a disciple of Baso (Matsu, d. 788), used to carry a cask of boiled rice at meal time before the monks' quarters loudly crying, 'Dinner is ready, O Bodhisattvas!' and burst out into a great laughter. For twenty years it is said he was in the habit of doing this. Engo comments (paraphrased): 'Tell me now what his idea is. If it is to announce the meal time there is the drum, there is the board, and the announcement is regularly given out. What is Kingyū's motive for bringing a cask of rice with him and making much fuss before the monks' quarters? Has he gone mad? If his intention is to give a sermon he should appear in the Dharma Hall and deliver it from the pulpit, properly prepared for the occasion. There is no sense in the master's behaving in such an unusual manner.' Engo goes on: 'There is evidently something in Kingyū's mind which defies speech, but which he wants somehow to communicate to the Brotherhood generally. His life is wholly devoted to this, he wishes to transmit what he has personally experienced to his fellow beings so that they can also share in the feeling he himself enjoys so much in the deepest part of his subjectivity.'

Secchō's versified comment runs:

> Enveloped in masses of white clouds,
> Peals of loud laughter we hear.
> Something is being delivered to us from both his hands:
> If one were [all-knowing] like a golden haired lion,

Even several thousand miles away,
One would detect what complicities are involved here.

Engo asks: 'What is Kingyū's message which is handed over to those Bodhisattva-monks? If what he holds in his both hands is not just a cask of boiled rice for their dinner, what is it? It must be something which defies the reach of language. What could it be? If a man were as old and experienced and wise as a golden haired lion, he would at once know what it is even if it is not openly delivered by means of laughter.'

In the following mondo,[1] the same laughter is heard though differently occasioned and between two knowing ones. Kyōzan (Yang-shan, 840–916) once asked Sanshō (San-shêng), disciple of Rinzai (Lin-chi), 'What is your name?' 'Ejaku (Hui-chi)', replied Sanshō. 'But that's my name', Kyōzan said, 'Yes, Enen (Hui-jan) is mine,' agreed Sanshō. And Kyōzan burst out into laughter.

Both Kyōzan and Sanshō understood Zen perfectly well, and knew each other as friends. Kyōzan's first question was intellectual or rather playful, perhaps wishing to have fun with him. Hence his question, 'What's your name?' Sanshō knew well what was in Kyōzan's mind, and answered Ejaku, instead of his own Enen. Kyōzan knew well what Sanshō had in mind. He simply and innocently said, 'That's mine.' Sanshō immediately responded without apology, 'Enen'. Both were sporting in the transcendental field of reality. Kyōzan naturally could not help laughing. Engo comments: 'His laughter is like a cool, refreshing breeze passing through the source of all things.'

Secchō's remark is:

The laughter's ended and whither vanished?
Throughout the ages it is likely to stir up a sad air.

Secchō is rather pessimistic here, thinking that posterity may fail to understand what was going on in the two masters' subjectivity. Or is it a sadness which comes from envy of their bliss?

To give another example of a master's hearty laugh: Yakusan (Yao-shan, 751–834) was a disciple of Sekito (Shih-t'ou). One evening he was climbing up the mountain for a walk when he suddenly saw the clouds open up and reveal a bright, shining moon, which made him burst out in a loud laughter. The cry was so loud that all the people within a distance of ninety *li* east of Li-yang heard it. After inquiries from door to door eastwardly the villagers finally were able to

---

[1] Mondo: literally 'asking and answering'.

trace it to Yakusan. Did the incident remind the master of the experience he had had at the time of enlightenment, which all of a sudden ushered him into the realm of the Infinite? The laughter must then indeed have come from the bottomless bosom of reality itself. Those who have the ear will be able to hear the master to this day.

Suiryō's laughter must have been of a somewhat similar nature to that of Yakusan. Suitō (Shui-lao), a disciple of Baso (Matsu), had a unique treatment from his master when he asked, 'What was the idea that prompted the first patriarch to come from the West (India) to the Middle Kingdom?' For the master without saying anything gave him a kick in the chest which made him fall to the ground. But when he got up from the toughest experience one could have as a result of simply wishing to be enlightened, he exclaimed rubbing his hands and giving out one of the heartiest of laughs, 'How wonderful! how wonderful! Thousands of samadhi containing the most profound mysteries can be seen in the tip of one hair right down to the very bottom of reality.' He made bows to the master and retired. Later, when he came to be at the head of a priory he used to say, 'Ever since I got a kick from my master my laughter has known no end down to this day.' It is said that when a monk asked him what the Buddha was, he laughed heartily.

6

As far as I can see, Zen is the only religion or teaching that finds room for laughter. Ordinarily if any one should declare that divinity may be eulogized by means of laughter, he would be called sacrilegious or considered a lunatic. But Zen has its own theory of laughter and the historical examples mentioned above are in accord with the spirit of Zen. Bergson is a great philosopher of modern times and his analysis of laughter is illuminating in this connection.

According to him, as I understand, the comic takes place essentially when some conscious restraints, moral or intellectual, are suddenly, unexpectedly, and absentmindedly removed, contradicting the content of the restraints. Restraints of whatever nature are habitually practised and acquire rigidity, inelasticity, automatism. When this artificial mechanization is somehow betrayed by 'some deep-seated cause, a certain fundamental absentmindedness, as though the soul had allowed itself to be fascinated and hypnotized by the materiality of a simple action', we have the comic. That is to say, when art is defeated by nature, when the art which is limited and finite is replaced by something infinite, beyond the calculation of human understanding, we are visited by laughter.

Bergson writes on the subject:

'Could reality come into direct contact with sense and consciousness, could we enter into immediate communion with things and with ourselves, probably art would be useless, or rather we should all be artists, for then our soul would continually vibrate in perfect accord with nature.'

The author seems to imply that we can never come to direct contact with reality and that the soul can never be in perfect accord with nature. Thus he tries to study the reason for this shortcoming on our part, and continues:

'We had to live, and life demands that we grasp things in their relations to our own needs. Life is action. Life implies the acceptance only of the *utilitarian* side of things in order to respond to them by appropriate reactions: all other impressions must be dimmed or else reach us vague and blurred. . . . My senses and my consciousness, therefore, give me no more than a practical simplification of reality.'

But let me ask: If it is 'a practical simplification of reality', does he know what reality in itself is? If he does not, how can he ever know what we see, what we hear, is no more than its simplification or generalization or selection? According to the author, however, our situation is worsened by our invention of speech:

'In short, we do not see the actual things themselves; in most cases we confine ourselves to reading the labels affixed to them. This tendency, the result of need, has become even more pronounced under the influence of speech; for words — with the exception of proper nouns — all denote genera.'

Bergson writes as if he is perfectly acquainted with 'the original life', for otherwise he could never have penned these passages. Enō (Hui-nêng), the sixth patriarch of Chinese Zen, is reported to have asked one of his persistent pursuers, 'Show me your original face which you had even before your parents gave birth to you.' This 'original face' is Bergson's 'original life' not only of the writer himself but also of 'the reporter' who writes all about the creation story as it is recorded in the Bible. Kierkegaard states, 'Truth is subjectivity'; this is a bold declaration and is in accord with the Buddhist statement, 'The triple world is my mind.' The Danish subjectivity and the Buddhist Mind are the same reality, the same original life, which we all generally as well as individually are in possession of. This is the Buddha's 'I' in 'Heavens above, earth below, I alone am the most honoured one!' and also God's, 'I am that I am.' When this Original I comes out of the darkening clouds of the hazy vapours of speech and logic, no one can help bursting into laughter. The I confronts infinity itself, no, the I is it, for God's isness is my isness, as proclaimed by Meister Eckhart. The Zen master keeps this I in the depths of his heart and lets it out constantly by means of his cryptography or ciphercode. 'Let those who have the ears to hear, hear it.' The laughter does not limit itself to a distance of ninety *li* of Li-yang, it extends even to the extremity of the heavenly galaxies.

Sengai's Hotei laughs this laugh and so do his Kanzan and Jittoku. It sweeps all over the cosmos like a refreshing breeze given out by Kyōzan's laughter. Hereby we also find pacified Kierkegaard's 'paradoxical passion of the Reason' (*Philosophical Fragments*, tr. by Swanson, p. 35) which is stirred when facing the Unknown, for the Unknown is now caught dancing over Kingyū's cask of boiled rice.

It may not be out of place here to add that Bergson's 'absent-mindedness' corresponds to Buddhist terms such as no-ego-ness (*muga, anātman*), no-thought (*munen*), or no-mind (*mushin, acitta*), everyday-mindedness (*heijō-shin*), just-as-it-is-ness (*jinen-hōni*), just-so-ness (*shimo*) as contrasted with artificially and consciously designed self-control or self-restraint.

7

In conclusion, I will give two more examples which express the feeling of joy the masters have in being in direct contact with reality, each in his own characteristic manner. They are highly informative in giving their happy appreciation of reality which they experience within themselves. No actual outburst of laughter is specifically recorded in these examples, but the readers can feel it by themselves — which is more interesting. The masters have no uniform method (*upāya*) whereby they strive to lead their pupils to the final personal understanding of things that are beyond relativistic intellectualization. They lived in surroundings different from ours, and it is natural that their pedagogical methodology differs from what we of modern times may adopt for our purposes. The fundamental principle does not change, but its application inevitably goes through changes. Sengai of the eighteenth century, living in the Tokugawa Era, found it most congenial to his character to express himself in the way he did as we see in the reproductions in the following pages.

Kwasan (Ho-shan, 891–960) used to give the following sermon which is in fact a quotation from the 'Book of Seng Chao', a great Buddhist scholar of the Six Dynasties. 'To discipline ourselves in learning is called ''hearing'', to reach the point where any learning no more avails is called ''approaching''. When one goes beyond these two stages, one is said to have truly transcended.'

Once a monk came out and asked, 'What then is ''truly transcending''?'

Kwasan, without uttering a word, motioned as if beating a drum, saying, 'Dong, dong, doko-dong, doko-dong!'

Another time, a monk asked, 'What is the truth itself?' Kwasan went through the same performance.

Another time, a monk asked, 'I would not ask anything about ''What is mind that is Buddha?'', but I should like to know what is meant by ''Neither mind nor Buddha''.' Kwasan's answer was as usual, 'Dong, dong, doko-dong, doko-dong.'

Another time, a monk asked, 'How would you treat one who is truly a man of super-understanding?' The monk was treated to the same performance as if the master was ignorant of any other kind of expression. The same 'Dong, dong, doko-dong' went on. Engo has his comments on this: 'An iron ball. An iron caltrop. Most assuredly held up.' 'But,' he continues, 'where does all this lead us? In the morning he (i.e., a man of super-understanding) is under the western sky and in the evening he is back in the eastern land.'

One may ask what relationship can all these statements have to Kwasan's beating the drum 'Dong, dong, doko-dong'? Is there anything good here, anything liable to evoke laughter on the part of anybody concerned here? It is in fact not Kwasan himself that plays the drum and laughs, it is 'the truth itself', it is 'the one who is neither mind nor Buddha, it is that which has truly transcended', that plays the drum and laughs. Is it not really good to see that each, though differently designated, goes through the wonderful performance?

Fuke (P'u-hua) was a contemporary of Rinzai (Lin-chi, d. 866) and helped Rinzai in his unique way to disseminate the teaching of Zen. He was a disciple of Banzan Hoshaku (P'an-shan Pao-chi). He behaved like a lunatic but his understanding was on the right track. Anyway, he remains a singular character in the history of Zen. In Japan he is regarded as having propagated the cult of the Komusō, 'Monks (or Followers) of Emptiness'. In the feudal days, they went about in a special costume and playing the flute called *shakuhachi* ('foot and eight').

When Rinzai came to the district of Hopei and settled at an unpretentious

14

temple by the River Hoti, Fuke was already in town and joined him. His whole life was eccentric and the people could not tell whether or not he was really of sane mind. He used to go about in the streets crying:

'Ming t'ou lai,
Ming t'ou ta;
An t'ou lai,
An t'ou ta;
Ssu fang pao mien lai,
Hsuan feng ta;
Hu kung lai,
Lien chia ta.'

The traditional sophisticated interpretation of the ditty is: If a man should come from the plane of relativity, he would be dealt with on the same plane. If he should come from the plane of the absolute, he would be so dealt with. If he should come irrespective of either plane, he would be dealt with in a whirlwind-like manner. If he should come from emptiness, he would be beaten back with a flail.

Rinzai learning of Fuke's behaviour, sent out one of his disciples with the following instructions: 'As soon as he finishes his song, grab him by the chest and demand an answer to the question, "What will you do with one who comes to you from none of the aforementioned directions?"'

When the disciple faithfully carried out Rinzai's instruction, Fuke released himself and said, 'There is a great feast tomorrow at the Daihi-in temple.' The disciple came back and reported to Rinzai all that happened. Rinzai, heartily approving, said, 'I was somewhat in doubt about his understanding. Now I realize thoroughly where he is.'

Fuke was intoxicated with Bergson's original life, as was Spinoza with his God. He did not laugh outwardly, but I feel that he was chuckling inwardly. I am again reminded of Sengai's Hotei (No. 113) who is in fact an image of Sengai himself.

8

Sengai was born the third son in the family of a farmer in the province of Mino in the central part of Japan. He had his head shaved and donned the monkish robe when he was eleven years old, the customary age for initiation in olden days.

At nineteen, his teacher permitted him to go on what is known as *angya*, a pilgrimage from one master to another. If the young man thinks he has found a good master for himself, he will decide to stay with him for some years, to carry on his study of Zen. Often, however, he may have already decided on the master before starting out on the journey. Sengai's choice was one of the great masters of the day who resided in Nagata near what is today the city of Yokohama. His name was Gessen Zenji.

Sengai's insight into Zen came when he understood the meaning of a story which was first told by a Chinese master of the T'ang named Kyōgen (Hsiang-yen); it is known as Kyōgen's 'Man on the Tree'.

The story goes like this. Kyōgen once gave a sermon: 'Here is a man hanging by his teeth on the branch of a tree. There comes a monk who asks him a question regarding the great principle of Buddhism. If the man does not answer the monk's question he is not a pious follower of Buddhism. If he opens his mouth to speak he will surely fall to the ground. What is your solution in this critical situation? Speak! Speak!'

Sengai stayed with Gessen for thirteen years, until the master passed away. He then started on his second *angya*. It is said that he travelled all over the central and the northern parts of Japan visiting various monasteries. For a while he settled in Mino, his native province. But the political conditions there did not please him, and he again left.

In the meantime, he received an invitation to come to Hakata, Kyūshū, where his senior monk-friend, who had also studied under Gessen Zenji, had his temple. Sengai accepted the invitation and settled at Shōfukuji where he became the abbot. At the time he was forty years old.

Shōfukuji was known for its being the first Zen institution to be established in Japan. It was founded in 1195, and Sengai was installed there as the one hundred and twenty-third abbot since its establishment. He was rightly elated at the privilege.

In 1811, at sixty-one, he retired from the abbotship of Shōfukuji, and spent the ensuing twenty years or so as a free man. It was principally during this time that he was most active as the people's friend, demonstrating his unique artistic talents, and expressing with wit and humour his deep Zen understanding. He was eighty-eight when his happy life came to an end.

He left many legends. There is one favourite story of how he once helped a younger member of his monastery. Sengai discovered that a disciple of his had the habit of leaving the monastic premises clandestinely during the night and quietly returning in the early morning. One morning, as the delinquent was crossing the fence back to the monastery, he set one foot on the other side and felt for the rock that usually served as foothold. This time, however, the stone felt soft and warm. Safely down on the other side, he soon recognized the figure of his master, Sengai, crouching low and doing his best to assure the safety of the monk's footing. The monk was beside himself with shame. Sengai, however, suggested that he should return to his quarters quietly with no further word on the matter.

'Sengai', occasionally abbreviated to 'Gai', is the *azana* by which he is best known. His given name (*imina*) is Gibon. Often, as the fancy struck him, he signed his calligraphies, ink-drawings or clay figures Hyakudō (one-hundred-hut), Kyohaku (empty-white), Muhōsai (no-rules study), Amaka Oshō (A-ma-hā priest), and so on.

INK DRAWINGS AND CALLIGRAPHIES
related to Sengai's life at the temples

佛會人天稱八萬　孔門子弟亦三千
山僧獨坐藤蘿石　時見浮雲過眼前
　　　　　　　　偶成

I. Sengai's Poem on Himself

The Buddha's congregation is said to have numbered
   eighty thousand;
Confucius, too, had disciples, as many as three thousand.
I sit alone on the vine-entwined rock
Occasionally looking at the clouds that pass by.

Buddha and Confucius were both great teachers of mankind, and we are all grateful for their love and wisdom. But how busy they must have found themselves, surrounded by so many disciples all crowding around them. The Indians are great at mathematics, though the Chinese are not far behind them. Three and eighty thousand are by no means small numbers. But here I sit idly passing away my time surrounded by white clouds. I have no followers, how fortunate I am!

This is Sengai's picture of his own life viewed subjectively. For objectively, though a retired abbot, he was surrounded by friendly callers from every station of social life; noble and humble, sick and poor, dissipates and drunkards, artists and scholars, men and women, religious and laity, young and old. He was kept busy responding to requests for poems, calligraphy and drawings. So often was he pestered by callers requesting his creations that he is said to have once stuck his head out the window to announce his own absence. The wonderful fact is that these accomplishments were employed in teaching worldly wisdom as well as morals.

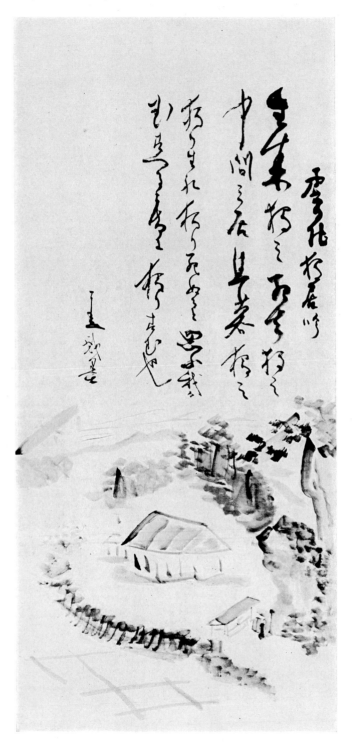

虚白院獨居吟
生来獨之　死去獨之
中間之居　旦暮獨之
獨り生れ獨り死ぬると思ふ我か
むすへる庵に獨りすむ也
　　　　　　　　　　　尾戯墨

22

II. Song of a Solitary Life at Kyohaku-in

> I come alone,
> I die alone;
> In between times,
> I'm just alone day and night.

> This I who comes to this world alone
> And passes away from this world alone —
> It's the same I who lives in this humble
>   hut all alone.

Elsewhere, Sengai adds:

> What I call alone
> Is to forget both alone and not-alone,
> And again to forget the one who forgets:
> This is truly to be alone.

Sengai's Song of Being Alone corresponds to Buddha's first utterance when he came forth from his mother's body: 'Heavens above and Earth below, I alone am the most honoured one.' This is the absolute affirmation, and every negation must finally come to this. Until it does, there will be no peace, no rest, not only with oneself but with the world. The modern world is trying to live in and with negations of all kinds. Hence this constantly tormenting anxiety.

We must never forget that empty nothingness is not the ultimate reality, that it has its positive aspect which is 'I am'. But 'I am' alone will never do. One must become conscious of 'I am' and 'I am' must be 'I am that I am'. Thus Eckhart states, 'God's isness is my isness,' and here we all have our final abode which is the 'no-abode' of Vimalakīrti.

孤筇山又水　興盡止奔馳
宁石苺苔古　春眠落日遲
　　　　　癸未之春
吾戲筆硯　非書非画
錯落人情　爲書爲画
　　淨妙禪師東輝菴写意図
　　並其一偈應荒木正受請
　　　　　　　洪厓拜

24

III. The View of Tōki-an

A sketch from memory of Tōki-an founded by Jōmyō the Zen Master, and a gātha (verse).

By request of Araki Shōju.

A solitary pilgrim [travelling] over hills
    and streams,
Wearily rests against his stick;
The steep crags are covered with aged moss;
The spring day is long and slumberous.
      Spring in the Year of the Sheep.

This play of mine with the brush and ink
Is neither [to be taken as] calligraphy nor drawing.
Yet in the hands of the common-minded people,
It becomes [mere] calligraphy and [mere] painting.
      Humbly,
      Kō-gai (Sengai)

遠　明　厓

IV. Far and Clear

A fine sample of Sengai's calligraphy. It was probably given to one of that countless stream of people who flooded his room with drawing paper, all asking for his calligraphy or ink-drawings. He jokingly remarked in one of his verses:

> They seem to think
> My study is a kind of toilet,
> They each come
> With a roll of paper.

紙數を娘に斗り頼まする　　　厓

V. The Girl with Paper

Sheets of paper,
Daughter only
Begging.

The meaning is not quite clear. The young daughter seems to be in the posture of reverently presenting sheets of paper to someone. It is likely that she has been sent by her parents to beg Sengai for more of his drawing or calligraphy. She had probably done this several times already and was ashamed of making another appearance.

こりや甚太良
虚白院へ行て
書ものねたるまいそ
摂譽取光居士
嘉永七年寅三月十四日湛元記

一升二升三升
北舟米や　崖

VI. The Rice Merchant

(*Left*)   'Look here, Jintarō! You are not to go to
                   Kyohaku-in and nag [the master] for calligraphy.'

It can be surmised from this drawing that the rice merchant, Jintarō, while he lived, was one who often troubled Sengai for his amusing pictures, and that Sengai drew this to rise to the situation. When Jintarō died, this painting was brought to the temple in order to have the Head Priest Tangen, Sengai's chief disciple and successor, inscribe Jintarō's Buddhist name and death date (top right-hand corner). It was then hung in the altar in lieu of the customary mortuary tablet. The inscription by Tangen reads: Setsuyō Shukō Koji, the 14th day of the third month, the 7th year of Kaei (1854).

(*Right*)   A Rice-measuring Box and a Leveller

One *shō*, two *shō*, three *shō*,
Kitafune the Rice Shop.

Formerly, in Japan, a square wooden box which held one *shō* or 1·588 quart was used to measure rice, and a wooden roller levelled off the excess grain. This is drawn by request of the rice-dealer Kitafune.

竹拾二枚陣瑚天鯛釣　　　厓
陣瑚一合辱御坐候　　厓

30

VII. Tiger and Cat

Twelve sheets of bamboo [drawings],
    This is fishing [a fine] sea bream with
      [a common] water flea.

                Gai

(In smaller letters):
    Thank you for the pint [container]
of rice-flour.

They say that there was once an old woman who greatly admired Sengai's paintings but being poor she had nothing of value to offer this high Buddhist dignitary in return for his drawings. One day, she came to beg Sengai for twelve paintings of bamboo, and in return she brought one *gō* (about half a pint) of rice-flour locally called *jinko*. Sengai playfully comments here that this is like fishing a sea bream (*tai*), the most valued fish in Japan, with a most common fish bait, the water flea, which is also called *jinko*.

Here the mighty tiger is meekly beating a retreat as he is being charged by a fiercely insistent cat. Observe the tiger's troubled expression.

The tiger is traditionally associated with bamboo.

31

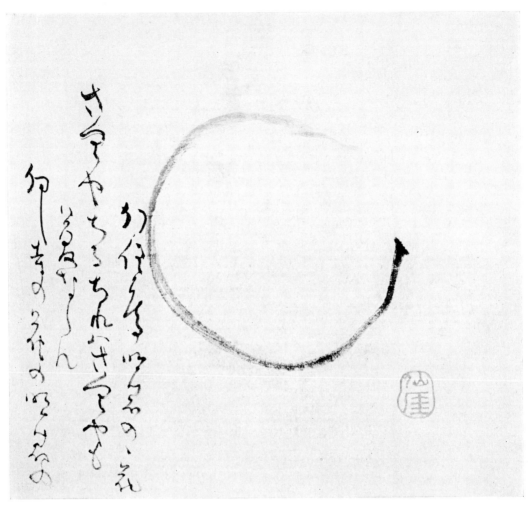

幻住庵明ほのゝ花
さくやちるちれハさくやも夢ならん
幻し寺の花の明けほの

VIII. Circle

The blossoms at dawn at Illusion-dwelling Cottage
Blooming and scattering,
Scattering and blooming,
'Tis all but a dream,
These flowers in dawn's twilight
At Illusion Temple.

Sengai's place of retirement was called Kyohaku-in (Empty-white-House) and Genjū-an, meaning Illusion-dwelling Cottage, was next to it.

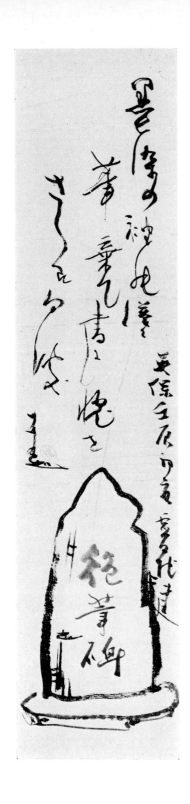

IX. Farewell Monument to the Brush

Erected at Kyohaku-in
Year of the Dragon of Tempō (1832)

This black-robed one abandons his brush
Into Sode-no-Minato (Harbour of Sleeves)
For the wind and waves to wash away
The shame of all his writings.

Sengai had a stone monument with these words erected in front of his hut, but he could not put an end to his 'unworthy' work, for no one would take his word seriously.

墨染の袖の湊に筆棄て
書にし愧をさらす白波
　　天保壬辰初夏虚白院建
　　　絶筆碑　　　　　厓

33

INK DRAWINGS AND CALLIGRAPHIES

○△□   扶桑最初禅窟

1. The Universe

The circle-triangle-square is Sengai's picture of the universe. The circle represents the infinite, and the infinite is at the basis of all beings. But the infinite in itself is formless. We humans endowed with senses and intellect demand tangible forms. Hence a triangle. The triangle is the beginning of all forms. Out of it first comes the square. A square is the triangle doubled. This doubling process goes on infinitely and we have the multitudinosity of things, which the Chinese philosopher calls 'the ten thousand things', that is, the universe.

The trouble with us linguistically-minded beings is that we take language realistically and forget that language is of no significance whatsoever without time. In truth, language is time and time is language. We thus come to think that there is in the beginning of the world a something which is real and concrete, such as a world of galaxies which though formless and nebulous is yet real and tangible. This is the foundation of the universe on which we now have all kinds of things, infinitely formed and varied. It is thus that time itself begins to be thought of as

36

something concrete and real. A circle turns into a triangle, and then into a square, and finally into infinitely varied and varying figures. In the same way the Biblical account of creation has turned into historical truth in the minds of many. But Zen is very much against such fabrications.

There is another and a more traditional interpretation that may be given to these three figures or forms. Sengai was familiar with Shingon, the *mantra* sect of Buddhism, as well as Zen. He liked Shingon because it taught the identity of the bodily existence (*rūpakāya*) with ultimate reality (*dharmakāya*). The bodily existence is here represented by a triangle which symbolizes the human body in its triple aspect, physical, oral (or intellection), and mental (or spiritual). The quadrangle represents the objective world which is composed of the four great elements (*mahābhūta*), earth, water, fire and air. The Dharmakāya, the ultimate reality, is the circle here, that is, the formless form. We generally hold a dichotomous view of existence, form (*rūpakāya*) and formless (*arūpa*), object and subject, matter and spirit, and think they contradict each other and are mutually exclusive. Both Shingon and Zen, however, oppose this view and hold that what is form is formless or empty (*śūnya*), that is, they are identical.

In his little treatise on this subject called *Tengan Yaku* (Medicine for the Eye), written in a dialogue form, Sengai estimates Zen as being higher than Shingon, and states that Zen is more direct and immediate and to the point without indulging in verbalism. Zen in this respect is the most effective medicinal drop for the eye that is still wandering on the level of intellection. It replaces this kind of eye with the one possessed by Mahāśvara (Great Lord). It is the divine eye which looks directly into the secrets of the ultimate reality. The opening or awakening to this order is abrupt and beyond verbal demonstrations of any sort, which is characteristically lacking in Shingon.

2. Amida Buddha

(Amida the Buddha of Infinite Light or Eternal Life)

Namu-amida-butsu

Amida is said to have meditated for five long kalpas; then, having decided what method (*upaya*) would be best to save all beings from going through a life of sufferings one birth after another, he spent ten more long kalpas to qualify himself for the task. He went through all forms of austerities performing self-sacrificing deeds of every possible kind. (A kalpa as a unit of time is practically the same as infinity.) Those who hold absolute faith in Amida and pronounce his name, *namu-amida-butsu*, once in all sincerity, will surely be born in the Pure Land of his. And this birth will not only ensure the total emancipation of the devotee himself, but also qualify him to return to this world of relativities and sufferings, and work for the spiritual welfare of all beings.

The inscription above the central figure of Amida contains some of the original prayers (*pūrva-pranidhāna*) proposed by Amida Buddha when he was still in the stage of Bodhisattvaship.

南無阿彌陀佛
文政戊子冬日　　扶桑最初禪窟隠人
　　　　　　　　　梵仙厓拜写

39

3. Buddha with His Attendants

Buddha is attended by two Bodhisattvas and sixteen arhats. The two Bodhi-sattvas are Samantabhadra (left) on an elephant and Mañjuśrī (right) on a lion. Samantabhadra, or Fugen in Japanese, symbolizes love or compassion (*karuṇā*) and Mañjuśrī, Monju in Japanese, transcendental wisdom (*prajñā*).

This is Sengai's rendering of a traditionally orthodox representation of Buddha with his usual group of attendants. It shows that Sengai was well schooled in the technique of the traditional style of painting.

4. Tripod

It is my constant thought:
The mind, Buddha, and all beings,
These three be undifferentiated.

かくの如く〜と思ふ我か
心佛衆　是三無差別 崖

The three legs or prongs united by a circle is the device to hold a kettle over the brazier charcoal fire. The Mind, Buddha, and all beings are one and not three — this is the teaching of Kegon philosophy. Sengai expresses in this Japanese poetic form his desire to practice the teaching in his daily life.

42

雪の山に昔し佛の見し星の
光リハ今にかわらぬものを
　　　　　　　　崖

5. Shākyamuni Coming Out of His Mountain Retreat

Over the snowy mountain [Himalayas],
The star is still shining
As ever brilliantly as when Buddha
    saw it long ago.
[But alas! some of us fail to see it.]

Shākyamuni, after leaving his home life in quest of the ultimate truth, spent six years studying philosophy and practising an ascetic life in a mountain retreat. But no light came to him. He became desperate, altogether at a loss what to do with himself. When he was in this state of mind he happened to look up, and saw the morning star, whose beams penetrated his whole being. He was awakened. Coming out of his retreat he set out to make the entire world acquainted with his experience so that they might share in the freedom he was enjoying.

43

轉法輪　　厓

6. Revolving the Wheel of Dharma

After several years of meditating in the mountain, Buddha came out from his retreat and gave his first sermon at Sarnath. This event is known in Buddhist history as the 'First Revolution', and Buddha's preaching activities are compared to the rolling of the wheel of the Dharma or Truth.

菩薩清凉月　遊於畢竟空
衆生心水淨　菩提影現中
世の憂きを心津くしに嘆けとて
我か衣てに波掛の岸
　文政丁亥十月
　　扶桑最初禪窟　梵仙厓拜画

7. Kwannon, Goddess of Mercy

The inscription on the extreme left reads:

The clear refreshing moon of
    Bodhisattvahood
Shines sportively in the sky of absolute
    Emptiness;
When the mind-water of ordinary
    beings is pure,
Enlightenment reflects itself on it.

Kwannon (Avalokiteśvara Bodhisattva) in Buddhism represents the compassion (*karuṇā*) aspect of Absolute Reality, and is resourceful in the practical display of this, her characteristic virtue, symbolically manifested in thirty-three forms. The picture here is one of such forms, known as the 'Water-moon Kwannon' (Suigetsu Kwannon).

On the bank of Namikake,
With my sleeves soaked in tears,
I sit deeply absorbed in contemplation
On the sorrows of human life.

The story of Kwannon is given in the section bearing the title *Fumon Bon* (Chapter on Universal Gate) in the *Lotus Sūtra* (*Hokke-kyō* or *Saddharma-puṇḍarīka* in Sanskrit).

世の憂きを心ろ津くしに嘆けとて
袖の湊に浪掛の岸　　　　匡拝戯

不動明王

46

8. Kwannon

Observing how badly the world is behaving, Kwannon, the Goddess of Mercy, is very grieved and her tear-soaked sleeves are as if soaked by the waves.

9. Fudō Myō-ō

Fudō Myō-ō (Acala-vidyā-rāja in Sanskrit) is one of the four Myō-ō (kings of knowledge) who are incarnations of the Buddha. All have fierce, angry, threatening features. They are meant to defend Buddhism against the attacks of evil spirits. Fudō, which means 'immovable', is the name of the king particularly favoured by the followers of the Shingon sect. The Shingon (Skt. *mantram*) is a form of Buddhism in which much of tantrism is incorporated.

Fudō holds a rope in his left hand and a sword in the right. The rope is to bind the evil passions that harass the mind and keep it from following the right path. The sword is to cut asunder all the ties that restrict the free movement of the original mind. The flames enveloping the whole body of the Myō-ō are to burn up every trace of defilement that prevents the human world from getting thoroughly purified. His sitting posture is the symbol of immovability. He sits adamantine, and nothing can affect his determined will to destroy everything that is impure and injurious to Buddhism. He is utterly devoted to fighting with evils, yet he remains serene in his inmost being, which is none other than the Dharmakāya itself. The Dharmakāya corresponds to the Godhead.

Elsewhere Sengai has this to say about Fudō Myō-ō:

> The right moment he knows
> To enter the world of pluralities;
> Like unto a mountain
> He sits immovable.

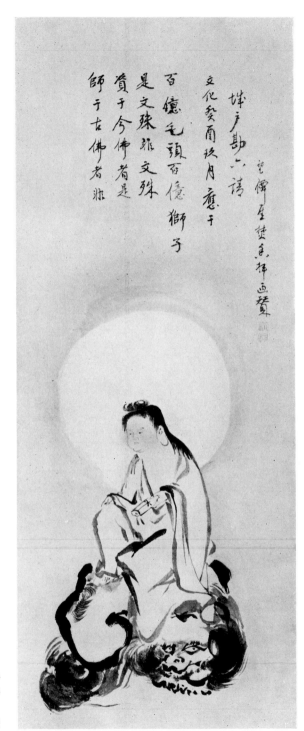

師于古佛者非
資于今佛者是
是文殊非文殊
百億毛頭百億獅子
文化癸酉玖月應于
城戸勘六請
梵僊厓焚香拜画賛

10. Mañjuśrī on a Lion

To be the teacher to the Buddhas of the past,
Is this not his properly assigned position?
[Or] to be helpful to the Buddhas of the present,
Is this his properly assigned position?
Whatever it may be, the Mañjuśrī here is not a historical
   Mañjuśrī.
At the tip of each hair on millions of lions
Are seen [dancing] millions of lions.

> In response to the request of Kido Kanroku, this 9th month of the Year of the Cock of Bunka (1813).

> With incense burning and respectfully bowing, this picture is drawn and the eulogy is inscribed by Bon Sengai.

The reference to the numberless lions on the tip of each hair of a lion symbolizes the Kegon philosophy of infinity. According to this, each object holds in it all other objects, infinite in number, not only summarily 'all in one and one in all', but there obtains also individually a state of universal 'interfusion'. This may lead us to think that the universe is in utter confusion. But we must remember that confusion implies individuality and assumes a state of things in which each is resisting the others. Kegon, however, holds that each individually retaining itself as such at the same time allows all others to enter it without there being any 'obstruction' (*muge*) between them.

文殊大士　厓

11. Monju Bosatsu

Monju Bosatsu or the Bodhisattva Mañjuśrī is the Bodhisattva of transcendental wisdom, *prajñā*, and one of the most important figures in the Mahāyāna system of Buddhist teaching. He is represented as holding a scroll of Buddhist texts in his left hand, while in his right he carries the sword of Vajrarāja. He rides on a lion, that strange looking animal Sengai has depicted here.

The significance of the scroll is self-evident, but the service his sword renders is twofold: one is to kill anything that would stand against the truth revealed to *prajñā* (transcendental wisdom, which is deeply lodged in the unconscious of every one of us); the other is to resuscitate the dead to a life they have hitherto never suspected. This double-functioned sword is in the hand of Monju. The sword is usually assumed to be a deadly weapon threatening with death and destruction anyone who thoughtlessly handles it; or symbolically it represents righteousness, justice and equity. But to the Mahāyāna followers the idea of love and creativity is more predominantly in it, especially when it is held by Monju.

The lion, the symbol of action and energy, is a significant figure in Zen texts. There are frequent references to the golden-haired lion whose roar can be heard throughout the universe, showing that Zen is not a gospel of quietude, as is sometimes thought, leading one to a realm of drowsy emptiness.

Monju (Mañjuśrī), Shākyamuni Buddha, and Fugen (Samantabhadra) make up one of the trinities of the Mahāyāna. Buddha sits at the centre, Monju to the left of him and Fugen to the right. Fugen, riding on an elephant, represents love and compassion, and enters into the world of particulars.

釋迦已歸雙林　彌勒未出内宮
甚矣吾衰也　不復夢見周公
　　　　　多羅菩薩画賛

52

12. The Yawning Hotei

Shākyamuni is long gone under the Twin Sala Trees;
Maitreya is still [in meditation] in the Tushita Heaven.
How aged I've grown now!
I have ceased to dream of the King of Chou!

Drawn and inscribed by Gai-tara
Bodhisattva (Sengai).

The inscription is filled with historical references. The first line refers to Shakyamuni Buddha who is recorded as having died two thousand five hundred years ago in India under two sala trees. Maitreya is a Bodhisattva, the future Buddha, who still resides in Tushita Heaven waiting to appear at the end of the present kalpa (a countless number of years). In the meantime there is no Buddha in this world but Sengai, who is already fully enlightened and who feels no need for the appearance of a Buddha. He is like Confucius who toward the end of his life told his disciples that he ceased to dream of the King of Chou as Confucius himself had already matured into a personality of his ideal, Chou Kung. Hotei, representing Sengai, is pictured as having just awakened from a fine doze.

出三界火宅露地座　　厓

13. Come out of the triple world [which is like]
a house on fire, and sit in the courtyard!

The parable of the house on fire is given in the *Lotus Sūtra*. The children inside the burning house, so thoroughly absorbed in their play, are unaware of the impending danger. The Buddha then devises a means to lure the innocents out of the house and into the open field where they may enjoy themselves to their heart's content.

負重涉遠　于人于天
吾已矣夫　無地息肩
　　　無端崖

14. Hotei

Carrying a heavy load and walking a long way
Among men, among gods,
I am all exhausted now.
Is there not a place where I can set the burden
　　down even for awhile?

55

七福を一福にして大福茶

15. The Seven Gods of Fortune

Have all the Seven Happinesses bundled up,
And out of them make One Happiness,
And out of it One Great Blissful Tea.

The six gods and one goddess of bliss, or the Seven Gods of Fortune, as arranged in this picture are from the top: God of Happiness, Wealth and Longevity (Fukūrokūjū); (left) God of Longevity (Jurōjin); Warrior God (Bishamon); Goddess of the Arts (Benzaiten); God of Plenty (Daikokuten); God of Wealth (Ebisu); and Hotei, the distributor of bottomless treasures, regarded as an incarnation of Maitreya. Hotei is shown here outstretched in great contentment. It is evident that this Bodhisattva was Sengai's favourite character.

龍女三千界　秦王十五城
斯珠人不眄　大黒闇中明

16. Daikokuten

This jewel which shines in the darkest of darkness
Is not at all noticed by people.
[It is the jewel for which] a Chinese king was willing
　　to part with fifteen of his towns;
[It is the jewel which] was presented to the Buddha by
　　a Nāga maiden, and which is said to be worth three
　　great chiliacosms.

Daikokuten, the God of Wealth, literally means 'very dark' or Mahākāla in India where he was primarily the great Hindu god of destruction. But in Japan he is the god of good fortune. He showers jewels called çintamani (as you will) from his wallet.

The Chinese king here refers to Duke Chao of Ch'in who, during the period known as the Warring States in China (403–221 B.C.), heard of the presence of a

58

jewel in the neighbouring dukedom called Chao. The Duke proposed to part with fifteen of his towns in exchange for the precious treasure, but the Duke of Chao refused to accept the offer. (See Ssu-ma Ch'ien's 'Records of History', *Shih-chi*, under 'Lin Hsing-jü'.)

The story of the Nāga maiden is found in the *Lotus Sūtra* under 'Devadatta'. It goes like this:

'When Mañjuśrī told the congregation about the subtle significance and the unfathomable truth of this "Lotus Sūtra", Prajñākuṭa asked, "Is there anyone who has ever penetrated into its deep meaning and finally attained Buddhahood?" Mañjuśrī answered, "Yes, there is one who is a Nāga maiden eight years old. She is the owner of the most excellently endowed intelligence and of a most compassionate heart. And it is she who would be a Buddha before long."

'Prajñākuṭa said, "That is impossible. Our Shākyamuni went through many eons of hard spiritual training before he attained to Buddhahood."

'Before he could finish with his sentence, the Nāga maiden herself appeared before them and first uttered her eulogy on the Buddha's virtues.

'Now Śāriputra said to the maiden, "You are a female who is said by her karma to be beset with five obstacles: 1. She cannot be a Brahma king; 2. She cannot attain the rank of Śakrendra; 3. She cannot be a devilish spirit; 4. She is debarred from becoming a lord of the whole world; and 5. She cannot obtain a Buddha-body. How can you aspire to the supreme enlightenment?"

'The Nāga maiden now took out a gem worth the whole universe and presented it to the Buddha, and the Buddha presently accepted it.

'Seeing this, the maiden spoke to Prajñākuṭa and Śāriputra, "I presented a gem to the Buddha who accepted it with no delay. Do you think it was quick?"

'They answered, "Yes, quick indeed."

'The maiden said, "With all your magical powers, you will see how quickly my attainment of Buddhahood will be."

'So saying, she immediately transformed herself into one of the male sex and in full possession of all the virtues of Bodhisattvahood and appeared in the world called Absolute Purity (*vimala*), sitting on the most finely decorated lotus flower. She was now seen fully endowed with a Buddha's thirty-two major and eighty minor marks and speaking on the Dharma to a large audience consisting of the various classes of beings and ultimately leading them to the supreme, perfect enlightenment.'

今歳から阿きなひ繁昌請合た

福ならは袋に入て貯へん
禍ひなら八槌て砕む

17. Ebisu and Daikokuten

(Left)   EBISU
Beginning with this year,
   Prosperous business guaranteed.

(Right)   DAIKOKUTEN
Should good luck come your way,
   I'll save it in my bag for you.
Should ill luck come your way,
   I'll crush it with my mallet for you.

From this we can well surmise that tradesmen came to Sengai for illustrated tokens with felicitous sayings on them. Sengai seems to have generously complied with their earthly desires and aspirations, perhaps with hopes of directing them towards doing good for the world generally.

These are two of the Seven Japanese Gods of Fortune. On the left is Ebisu in his customary fisherman's garb, and Daikokuten is on the right with bales of rice under his feet, carrying a magic mallet and a huge bag.

Ebisu is quite likely an imported god, for his name *ebisu* means foreigner, or a person from outside the Japanese boundaries. His fisherman's outfit also indicates that he is connected with life on the sea.

Daikokuten also is of foreign origin. Daikoku corresponds to the Hindu god Mahākāla, 'the great-black', or 'great-darkness'. He is an incarnation of Shiva as destroyer, black and of a terrifying aspect. In Japan he has turned into a god of luck. When Daikokuten shakes his magic mallet, there will be a shower of jewels called *cintamani*. To the holder of the jewel, every wish he may cherish will be granted.

18. The Star of the South Pole

A hundred men, each a hundred
   years old,
Together, they make ten
   thousand years;
Still the number is a limited
   one.
So towards the Star in the
   Southern Sky they go,
[In quest for eternal life].

    According to ancient Chinese astronomy, there lies a fixed star in the southern heavens corresponding to the North Star. It symbolizes longevity and is popularly represented by Jurōjin, one of the Seven Gods of Fortune, who is shown as an old man with a pointed head and a long beard.

百歲百人　都一萬年
猶是有限　故迎南星於天
　　　　　　　　庄應請

62

世の中に福寿そろふた人もな志
上長かけれハ下もハ短か志　厓

19. Fuku-roku-ju

Fuku-[roku-]ju,
Not a soul in the world
Is in possession of all three:
If the top is long,
The bottom is short.

Fuku is luck, *roku* wealth, and *ju* longevity. These three are the ideals of the Chinese people as individuals. To be blessed is to be blessed with enough children so that the ancestral line may be continued and their spirits be remembered for ever by posterity. The Chinese life revolved about the virtue of filial piety. I wonder how their present political régime suits this age-old tradition. To be wealthy means to be economically secure. Longevity is generally represented by a long-headed old gentleman seen here as having a relatively shorter pair of legs.

Sengai, being a good Buddhist, warns the worldly people not to be too greedy in trying to satisfy all their desires. Contentment is a far better virtue.

63

福の神福ハ釣るとも毒くふな　　崖

20. Ebisu

May the God of Luck (*fuku*)
Fish up *fuku* (good luck).
And not the poisonous one.

Ebisu is one of the Seven Gods of Fortune, generally represented with a smiling face and a pair of big ears. He is dressed like a fisherman, carrying an angling rod and a big sea bream (*tai*), which symbolizes a happy occasion (*medetai*).

Fuku, usually *fugu*, is a globefish that puffs out its belly into a ball when irritated. As food it is said to be delicious, but it is poisonous unless properly cleansed of its toxic parts. As *fuku* in Japanese also means good luck, Sengai plays on the double meaning of the words. He hopes Ebisu does not make a wrong catch. The wiser thing is to be above all luck, good or bad, but the wisest thing of all, is to hope for good luck, for the hope helps it to come, a little.

64

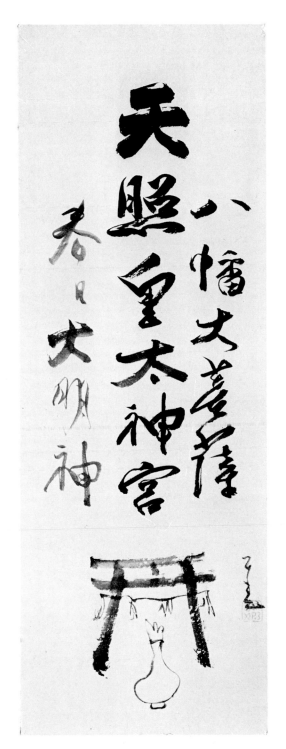

21. A Trinity of Japanese Gods

(*Centre*)
Ama-terasu-kō-tai-jin Gū
(The Shrine of the Heaven-illuminating-
     great-august-god)
     (*Right*)
Hachi-man-dai-bo-satsu
(Hachiman the Great Bodhisattva)
     (*Left*)
Kasu-ga-dai-myō-jin
(Kasuga the Great-illuminating-god)

These three are some of the most popularly worshipped gods in the Shintō hierarchy. Sengai was interested in the traditional Shintō teaching. Hachiman is the guardian god of the Genji family, while Kasuga is the protector of the Fujiwara family. It is significant that Hachiman is given the Buddhist title of 'Mahā-bodhisattva' or the great being of wisdom. When Buddhism was introduced into Japan, efforts were made to assimilate Shintō, the indigenous faith, into the Buddhist body, and often the Shintō gods were regarded as incarnated Bodhisattvas.

八幡大菩薩
天照皇太神宮
春日大明神
　　庄

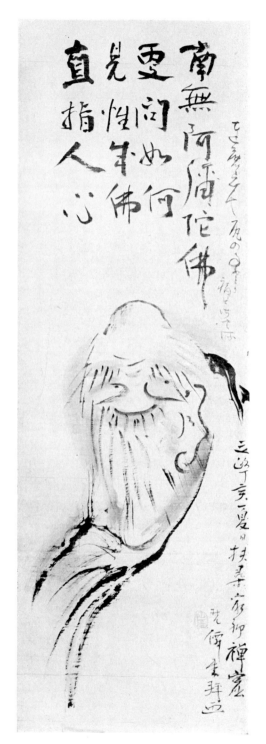

直指人心　見性成佛
更問如何　南無阿彌陀佛
　　達磨忌や尻の年ふとか痛と御坐流
　　文政丁亥夏日
　　　扶桑最初禅窟　梵僊崖拜画

22. Bodhidharma

Directly pointing to the human mind,
[He has us] see into the Essence
And attain to Buddhahood.
[But if you further insist on]
Asking questions,
[I would say,]
Namu-amida-butsu!

Solemnly, Sengai writes in classical Chinese a tribute to Bodhidharma, the first patriarch of Zen Buddhism in China. The first three lines are often quoted by Zen people as constituting the principle of Zen discipline. However, if there is anyone who wants further to know what 'the Essence' is, the answer given is: 'Namu-amida-butsu'. This is a mantram-like phrase which, in the original Sanskrit, means 'Devotion to the Buddha of Infinite Light (or Eternal Life)'. It is repeatedly pronounced by the followers of the Pure Land School of Buddhism and reminds us very much of the 'constant prayer' practised by the Russian Orthodox Christians. Sengai treats it here as a kind of Zen *kōan*.[1]

Bodhidharma is believed to have come to China from southern India circa A.D. 470 and to have died A.D. 528. In the Zen monasteries, the monks commemorate his death-day by devoting part of that day to formally sitting cross-legged in meditation.

Along the edge of the scroll Sengai has a seventeen-syllable haiku verse:

The Memorial Day of Bodhidharma is come,
And I sit in meditation,
But Oh! the pain of that boil on my buttock!

Reverentially drawn and inscribed by Bon Sengai of the first Zen Institution of Japan, this summer day, in the second *stem* of the element Fire of the Year of the Boar,[2] Bunsei (1827).

---

[1] A kind of question given the Zen student. See Suzuki's *An Introduction to Zen Buddhism* (London, Rider & Co., 1948, pp. 99–117).

[2] This refers to the cyclical system of Chinese chronology.

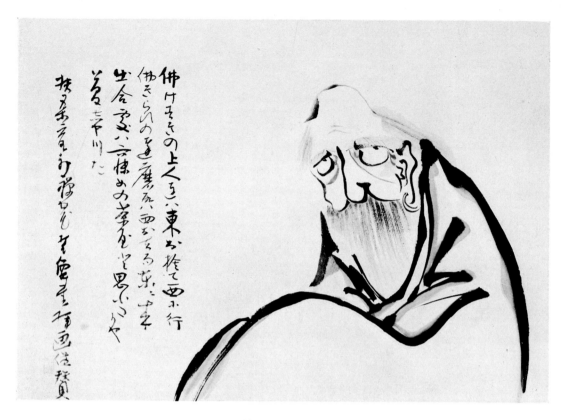

23. Bodhidharma (Daruma)

Those honourable Buddhist scholars who love Buddha, leaving the East go westward [that is, to India]; Mr. Daruma who dislikes Buddha, leaving West, comes eastward. I thought they might meet at the tea-house of awakening. But, woe is me! it was all a dream.

This satiric comment on Buddhists is characteristic of Sengai. The idea is that those who jealously cling to Buddha's words always look towards Buddha as the sole authority, whereas Bodhidharma or Daruma, who upholds the meaning of Buddha's words instead of the words themselves, has left India and settled in the Far East. As the one goes eastward and the other in the opposite direction, they are likely to meet at a certain point, which is no other than the enlightenment experience. But strangely enough, those who are scholars will stick to words, and those whose pride is in 'experiencing' the truth despise the study of literature. Do they not know that learning as well as the enlightenment experience is needed?

[Drawing 23]

24. Bodhidharma as a Woman

Pray, look at me:
A pseudo-transformation of Daruma.

達磨のはけ物
見てくれなんセ

Bodhidharma is the first patriarch in the history of Zen in China. He is said to have brought Zen from India in the fifth century, though, to be accurate, the history of Zen so-called does not begin until Enō (Hui-nêng, 638–713). The story of Bodhidharma (Daruma in Japanese and Ta-mo in Chinese) is wrapped in all kinds of legends. Zen people follow the belief that he had an interview with the Emperor Wu of the Liang and later retired into the mountains where he spent nine years deeply absorbed in meditation.

He is usually portrayed with a prominent nose, overhanging eyebrows, and a heavy beard. Most probably, not being used to the severe climate of northern China, he must have covered his head and body with warm clothing. Sengai has put him in the guise of an enticing woman here.

短か夜を眠りころんで起き上り

25. Bodhidharma

The night is short,
And I rise from lying flat on the floor
Like an *okiagari* doll.

This figure is known as the *okiagari-koboshi*, literally 'a little sitting-up monk', and represents Bodhidharma, the first patriarch of Chinese Zen. In Japan, Bodhidharma, or Daruma in Japanese, took on an interesting transformation, becoming a doll which was popularized to such an extent that few people today suspect the origin of this figure to whom we of the East owe so much. Usually made of papier-mâché, it is a self-righting toy so that however much one may try to knock it down, it will always regain its upright position. 'Seven times down, but up on the eighth', is the saying in connection with the *okiagari-koboshi* which is a model of patience, of steadiness, not giving up, or imperturbability. The dignified Bodhidharma is said to have spent nine long years unmoved in deep meditation facing the wall in northern China. Today he lives in the form of this tumbling toy close to the Japanese heart.

本邦佛門棟梁　聖德太子　崖

26. Prince Shōtoku

Prince Shōtoku, Leader of Japanese Buddhism

Shōtoku Taishi (574–622) is one of the greatest figures in the early history of Japan. He was great not only personally, but also as a statesman, philosopher, historian, organizer, and even as an architect. He is entitled to the last qualification as the one who supervised the building of the Hōryūji Temple in Nara. It still remains as an immortal monument to his genius. In those early days of Japanese civilization, one who could have conceived the idea of such a splendid specimen of architecture must be regarded as the owner of an extraordinarily gifted mind. Of course, he was not the designer but the one who, as the person in authority, gave the sanction to carry out the plan. It is no wonder that among Japanese carpenters he is worshipped as the god of their profession.

The Prince was also eminent as a philosopher who mastered all the subtleties of the deep metaphysical thought which developed in India and came through China to Japan. This deep thought was conveyed by means of the complicated Chinese characters, which the Prince could not only read but could freely use to express himself. He was a commentator of the three great Mahāyāna texts: The *Saddharma-Puṇḍarīka Sūtra*, *Vimalakīrti Nirdeśa Sūtra*, and the *Śrīmālādevī-Siṃhanāda Sūtra*.

In his 'Fundamental Law of Seventeen Articles', the Prince gives the moral principles of the government and of the Japanese people, emphasizing the law of harmony as most essential in our social life.

千光　葉上　兩朝賜号
合呼吾門初祖
　　　　　厓拜筆

27. Eisai

Senkō and Yōjō
Were titles bestowed by two emperors.
Put them both together
And you have the name of our first father.

Eisai (1141–1215) was the first transmitter of the Rinzai Zen sect of Buddhism to Japan. He is known for having established Kenninji Temple in Kyoto, Jufukuji in Kamakura, and Shōfukuji in Hakata prefecture where Sengai held abbotship. Eisai was also learned in the Shingon (Mikkyō) sect of Buddhism, and it is likely that Sengai, too, followed the founder's example in studying Shingon.

Senkō, or 'one thousand rays of light', was the title posthumously given Eisai, and it refers to a legend told of him. Once, during Eisai's first journey to China, a great drought took place and the local governor asked Eisai to pray Heaven for rainfall. It is said that as Eisai performed this prayerful ceremony a thousand rays emanated from his body, and the ritual averted disaster.

Yōjō was another posthumous title, and is the name of one of the branches of the Tendai-Shingon school which Eisai originated.

Eisai visited China twice, the first being a short stay in 1168, and the second lasting five years from 1186 to 1191. Today, he is perhaps best recalled for having introduced the tea plant to Japan.

打爺拳子

一喝三日

76

28. Baso and Rinzai

(*Right*)   One 'Kwatz!'[1] [and] three days.
(*Left*)   The fist that strikes the father.

These two pictures illustrate the most remarkable incidents recorded in the history of Zen in China. The first phrase refers to the event that took place between Baso (Ma-tsu, 709–88) and his disciple Hyakujō (Pai-chang, 720–814). Hyakujō was coming for his second visit to Baso. Baso seeing him approach took up the *hossu*[2] from his chair and produced it before Hyakujō. Hyakujō then said:

'This act itself? Or apart from this act?'

Baso said nothing. He placed the *hossu* back where he got it.

Baso remained seated for a while, and resumed, 'What would you do after this when some one accosts you and asks what Buddha-dharma is?'

Hyakujō took up the *hossu* and produced it before him.

Baso now asked, 'Apart from this act?'

Hyakujō returned the *hossu* where it belonged.

Baso uttered, 'Kwatz!'

The utterance is said to have rendered Hyakujō deaf for three days.

'The fist that strikes the father.' This is what happened when Rinzai (Lin-chi, d. 866) returned to his master after getting his satori under Daigu (Tai-yü). Rinzai is one of the great Zen masters of the T'ang era, and the school bearing his name is still thriving in Japan. When still young, he applied himself with his whole being to the mastery of Zen. Before this, he had studied the Vinaya texts and also the philosophical works on Buddhism; but they had failed to satisfy him. He came to Ōbaku Kiun (Huang-po Hsi-yün, d. 850) and stayed with him three years, but nothing happened to him. Bokuju (Mu-chau), an elder member of the Brotherhood, advised him to go directly to the master and ask, 'What is the essential teaching of Buddhism?' Rinzai following this advice approached Ōbaku and asked as he was instructed by Bokuju. But what he got from the master was just a blow of the stick with which he was driven away. This occurred three times. Rinzai thereby became impatient and wished to go elsewhere.

[1] 'Kwatz!' is an unintelligible ejaculation uttered by the Zen master.
[2] A *hossu* was originally a mosquito-swatter. It is now a religious insignia for a Zen master or a high cleric.

Bokuju again told him through Ōbaku not to go anywhere else but to Daigu (Tai-yü) who would be able to lead him to enlightenment. The faithful Rinzai saw Daigu and told him all about his experience under Ōbaku. Daigu said, 'What a grandmotherly master Ōbaku is! And you come here asking me where you are at fault. You stupid fellow!' This reproachful comment opened his mind all of a sudden to a state of enlightenment which made him exclaim, 'After all there is not much in Ōbaku's teaching!'

Daigu now seized him and demanded, 'What do you mean by making such a remark? When you first came to me you wanted to know where you were at fault; and now you utter such a shameless remark, "There is not much in Ōbaku!" What are you talking about? Explain yourself, quickly!'

Rinzai, instead of giving any real response, poked Daigu in his side three times. Daigu now let him go, saying, 'After all, Ōbaku is your teacher, and I have nothing to do with you. Begone!'

When Ōbaku saw Rinzai coming back, he said, 'What makes you come back so soon?' Rinzai said, 'It is all due to your grandmotherly kindness that I am here again.' Thereupon Rinzai told Ōbaku all about what happened between Daigu and himself. After listening to his story, Ōbaku burst out, 'When I see that fellow, I will surely give him a good slap in the face!' Rinzai responded at once, 'Why wait so long? You can have it yourself this moment.' So saying, Rinzai lost no time in slapping his master in the face. This is the 'striking the father'.

From examples like this, one can see that there is something in Zen that makes one feel the utter inadequacy of verbalism. Verbalism is conceptualism and conceptualism is like handling things with gloves which always keep us away from realities. This is one of the reasons why the Zen masters resort to the use of a stick or a fist. Zen is not to be identified with a merely psychological or medical treatment.

29. The Master and the Cat

Cut one, cut all,
The cat is not the only object.
Let them all be included,
The head-monks of the two dormitories,
And even Wo the Old Master.

Wo (Wang) was the family name of Nansen Fugwan (Nan-ch'üan Pu-yüan, 748–834), one of the great disciples of Baso (Ma-tsu). He is often referred to as 'Wo the Old Master'. Sengai's verse of general slaughtering refers to the famous story of the cat whose ownership was disputed between the east and the west dormitories in Nansen's monastery. The head monks of the two quarters then went to the Old Master to have the matter settled once and for all. The Master held up the object in question high before the whole congregation and declared: 'If there is any among you, O Brethren, who could say an appropriate word for this momentous occasion, speak out. Otherwise, the cat might have to lose its life.' Seeing that nobody could rise to the occasion, it is believed that the Master cut the cat in two.

When toward the evening Jōshū (Chao-chou), a leading disciple, came back, Wo the Master told him about the incident during the day and asked him what he would have done. Jōshū, who just happened to be removing his travelling sandals, took one of them and put it over his head and went out. Seeing this, the Master said, 'Too bad that you were not with us, for you could have saved the poor cat.'

This is one of the most interesting stories in the annals of Zen. The question is not how far the legend contains elements of the fact. What the Old Master wanted us to see here was whether the disputing disciples could go beyond the limits of dualistic-mindedness or philosophical intellection. Sengai knows well what the Old Master was after and faithfully follows in his footsteps in proposing a total cleaning up of the stale house erected by logicians or semanticists.

日本風　寒山拾得　　厓

30. Kanzan and Jittoku

Kanzan and Jittoku, Japanese style

Kanzan (Han-shan) and Jittoku (Shih-tê) are favourite subjects of Zen painters and poets, and in this Sengai was no exception. The story of the two Chinese hermit-poets appear in the *Dentōroku* (*The Transmission of the Lamp*, fas. 27). They flourished probably early in the ninth century. Their poems are collected in a book known as the *Kanzan-shi* or *Sanrai-shu*, the bulk of which are Kanzan's. The two are true symbols of the undying free spirit of creativity.

80

茶　果
趙州喫茶去　雲門胡餅已
扶桑最初禅窟　厓書

31.　Tea and Cake:
The tea is served by Jōshū;
The cake by Ummon.

Master Jōshū (Chao-chou, 778–897) once had two monk visitors. He asked them if they had been there to see him before. One monk answered, 'No, I have not.' Jōshū said, 'Have a cup of tea.' The other replied, 'Yes, I have.' To this Jōshū gave the same salutation: 'Have a cup of tea.'

There was a keeper of the temple who approached Jōshū and asked, 'You seem to treat the monks in the same manner whether they respond with a yes or a no. How is this, O Master?' Without replying, Jōshū called, 'O my friend!' And the keeper answered, 'Yes, Master.' And Jōshū said, 'Have a cup of tea!'

Ummon (Yün-mên, 864–949), another Chinese Zen master, was once asked, 'What is the subject all Buddhas and Patriarchs talk about?' This is tantamount to asking, 'What is the transcendental truth that defies all description?' Ummon simply said, 'A piece of pastry.'

Sengai tells us to drink Jōshū's tea and eat Ummon's cake if we wish to experience the teaching which is given by all the Buddhas and Patriarchs, that is, Zen. (See Plate No. 119.)

點那這心　過現未来
吹滅紙燭　金剛爲灰
　　　　　厓道者拜画

32. Ryūtan and Tokusan

What mind do you punctuate?
The past, present, or future?
The candle is blown out,
And the *Diamond* turns to ashes.

The story behind this inscription is this: When still a youth and not yet initiated into Zen, Tokusan (Tê-shan, 782–865) prided himself on knowing much about the Vinaya texts and various treatises on the 'Diamond Sūtra'.[1] Upon hearing of Zen and its radical interpretation of Buddhism, he headed southward, where Zen teaching prevailed, determined to crush this unorthodox school of Buddhism.

At a roadside tea-house he wished to have some refreshments. In Chinese, a repast of this sort is called *tien-hsin*, literally, 'punctuating the mind'. The old woman-keeper of the house seeing Tokusan with a bundle on his back, asked what he had in it. 'Seiryō's commentary on the "Diamond Sūtra",' said Tokusan proudly. Then the old woman said, 'I have a question to ask you. If you answer it satisfactorily, I will serve anything you ask, on the house. Otherwise, I must ask you to leave and go elsewhere for your refreshment. According to the Sūtra, neither the past mind nor the present mind nor the future mind is attainable. This being the case, pray tell me, which mind do you wish to "punctuate"?' Tokusan failed to answer her question, and was forced to go hungry. The old woman-keeper knew something of Zen.

When Tokusan reached his destination, Ryūtan (Lung-t'an), he studied Zen hard under the leadership of Sōshin (Ch'ung-hsin), the master at Ryūtan. One day while he was attending his master, the latter said, 'It is late, why not return to your own quarters?' Tokusan went out and noticed that outside it was already dark. 'It is dark,' he said to his master, who passed a lighted candle over to him. But when Tokusan was about to receive it, the master suddenly blew it out. This is said to have brought Tokusan's mind to a full awakening.

Sengai's comment 'The *Diamond* turns into [a pinch of] ashes' refers to this incident in the life of Tokusan, who was noted in the history of Zen as a great wielder of the stick. One of his famous sayings is: 'Whether or not you ask a question, you get thirty blows of my stick.' (See Plate No. 37.)

[1] One of the Buddhist canonical books belonging to the Prajñāpāramitā class which essentially discusses the problem of Prajñā, the transcendental wisdom.

33. The Turnip

Turnips and Zen monks,
Are [both] best when they sit
well.

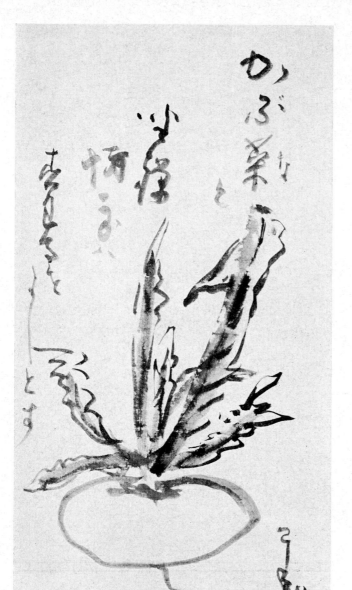

かぶ菜と坐禅坊主ハ
すわるをよしとす　　厓

Turnips are best-tasting when they are plump and somewhat flat at the seat. Zen monks are best qualified for further training when they are able to sit well in the cross-legged posture of deep meditation.

千寺らへて法の華問鶯
木末擇てなき渡る哉　厓

34. Travelling Monk

Flying from temple to temple
Asking for the floral essence of the Dharma,
O nightingale!
You know what branch to choose
And go on singing your song!
[*Hō, hokke-kyō, hō hokke-kyō!*]

The nightingale is supposed to sing *hō-hokke-kyō! hō-hokke-kyō!* which is the title of one of the most important Mahāyāna sūtras expounding the fundamental Dharma, the truth. *Hō* is Dharma, *ke* flower, and *kyo* sūtra. In full, it runs *Myōhō Rengekyō* (*Saddharma-puṇḍarīka-sūtra* in Sanskrit). It is also known as the *Lotus Sūtra*.

The pilgrim is compared to the nightingale.

85

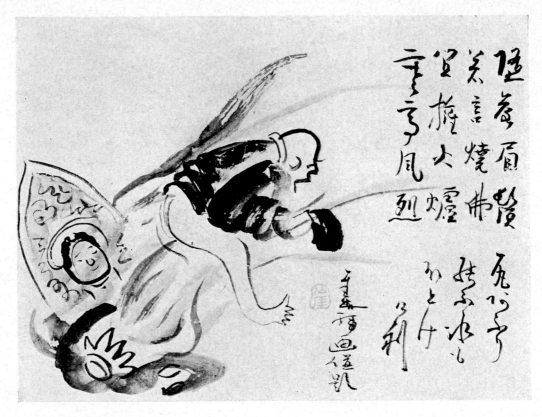

寒高風烈　宜擁火爐
若言燒佛　堕落眉鬚
尻阿ふり結ふ氷もほとけ々利
　　　　　厓拜画佽題

35. Tanka Burning the Buddha Image

The wind is high, the cold is penetrating;
The fire must be stirred up in the hearth.
If you call this 'burning the Buddha',
You will see your eyebrows as well as your
    beard falling off.

The hip is warmed now,
The hard ice is melting.
Here is the Buddha (*hotoke*).

This is the story of the Zen monk Tanka Tennen (Tan-hsia T'ien-jan, 739–824) who one evening was staying at Erinji Temple in the capital. Finding it severely cold, he took down one of the wooden figures of the Buddha from the altar and made himself a fire with it. When the temple keeper learned of this, he exclaimed, 'Why did you commit such an outrageous deed?' Said Tanka quietly, 'I wished to collect the *śarīra*.' *Śarīra* is the remains of a cremated Buddha or a holy man, often in the form of bones or pebble-like matter. 'How absurd to try to find *śarīra* by burning a wooden statue!' said the keeper, to which Tanka retorted, 'If so, then may I not have another one to burn?'

This apparently horrible and sacrilegious conduct on the part of Tanka did not affect him in any form, physical or spiritual, while the temple keeper is said to have suffered the retribution of having his beard and eyebrows fall off. The falling off of the beard is generally considered a kind of spiritual punishment.

Sengai, in his Japanese verse, has a pun on the word *hotoke* which may mean Buddha, or, as a verb, to melt, to release, or to be free from bondage. Tanka, a free man, is a Buddha, and what retribution can come of one Buddha burning another Buddha, which in Tanka's case was no more than a wooden figure?

一箇魁芋
十年猶嗅
　　厓

36. The Taro-baking Monk

One big head of taro,
The smell lasting ten years.

The monk is Ransan (Lan-tsan or Tsan the Lazy), and the story is about the interview he had with the imperial messenger. Myōsan (Ming-tsan) was his real name, but not being fastidious about the details of daily affairs as his mind was too absorbed in transcendental things, his brother-monks called him Tsan the Lazy. Ransan's virtue of unworldliness came to be widely talked about, and the rumour finally reached the Chinese T'ang Emperor Tokusō (Tê-tsung, reigning 779–805). He sent a messenger to have Ransan brought to his court.

The messenger found Lan-tsan baking a taro-head in a fire made of dry cowdung. The monk paid no regard to the court dignitary, who had announced the object of his visit. As Ransan pulled his food out of the ashes, the messenger noticed his running nose. He called Ransan's attention to it and advised him to wipe himself. Ransan retorted, 'How am I to find time to interrupt myself just to please a layman's whim?'

The messenger returned to the court and reported his failure to get the monk-recluse. At this the emperor's respect for the Lazy Tsan was heightened all the more.

Ransan's simple spirit, his devotion to a life of Tao to which worldly glory meant less than nothing, that is the smell of his baking-taro, as its saintly scent for ever more permeates down through the centuries.

道得不得　総三十棒　　　　　　　　諸方火葬　這裏活埋

37. Tokusan and Rinzai

These are two great Zen masters of the T'ang dynasty, China. Tokusan (Tê-shan, 782–865), on the left, was noted for swinging his stick somewhat liberally; whereas Rinzai (Lin-chi, d. 866) used to come out with an unintelligible ejaculation — Kwatz! — whenever a monk approached him with a question. In this picture Tokusan is as usual represented with the stick and his favourite statement:

> Whether you speak or do not speak,
> Thirty blows of my stick,
> Just the same!

The idea is to transcend contradiction, opposition and dualism of all kinds by identifying it. This is logically impossible, but Tokusan would say that we are acting it in our daily life. Zen is the art of making us conscious of this fact or truth by actual experience. Tokusan is a veteran Zen master; his stick has nothing to do with the giving of shock treatment to mentally disturbed patients, as is often imagined by modern readers. It is meant to wake a sound-minded truth-seeker to a state of spiritual self-consciousness.

Rinzai (right) utters his 'Kwatz!' as Tokusan uses his stick. Here he carries a spade. One ordinary working day, Rinzai was out with the other monks tilling the ground. Seeing Ōbaku his master approaching, he stood up, leaning on his spade. Ōbaku said, 'Is this fellow tired?' Rinzai replied, 'The spade is not yet lifted up, how could he be tired?' Ōbaku struck him. Rinzai took hold of the master's stick and pushed both it and Ōbaku to the ground. Ōbaku called out to the overseeing monk to help him up. The monk as he did so, said, 'Why do you allow this lunatic to treat you so rudely?' Whereupon Ōbaku struck the overseer. Rinzai remarked as he dug the earth:

> At all other places they cremate them;
> Here we bury them alive!

The Zen method of training is unique and has no parallel in the world history of spiritual exercises. It is most drastic; there is no half-killing. The killing is to be so complete that there will be a rebirth. The half-dead can never be resuscitated. The crucifixion must be thorough. Otherwise Christ will never rise again, and paradise will never be regained. Rinzai knows all this from his experience. Hence his statement.

91

古人刻苦　我目如眉
若言臨済出常情
猶是腦門欠一錐
　　　　崖杜多拝画偬題

38. Jimin and the Drill

The ancient master trained himself mercilessly.
My eyes are like the eyebrows.
He may say 'Rinzai goes beyond ordinary sense,'
But [I say that Jimin] still needs another piercing
　　drill into his brain.

Jimin (Tz'u-ming, 987–1040) was one of the great Chinese Zen masters of the early Sung. While disciplining himself in the study of Zen, he often used a drill to prick his thigh to keep from feeling drowsy in practising meditation (*zazen*). When he finally attained enlightenment he remarked: 'I now know that Rinzai (Lin-chi, founder of the Rinzai School of Zen) goes beyond ordinary sense.'

Sengai wants to warn us that though Jimin speaks here of 'beyond the ordinary', there is after all nothing extraordinary in Zen. When tired, I sleep; when hungry, I eat. Are not these acts most miraculous and at the same time most common? Sengai tells us to keep both feet planted firmly on the ground. The last line draws our attention to this point in a typically Zen fashion. The second line is not quite clear.

92

詩向會人吟　酒逢知己吞

39. Kanzan and Jittoku

Poems are to be read to those who understand them,
While saké is to be taken with one who knows you.

The two good friends, Kanzan (Han-shan) and Jittoku (Shih-tê) probably lived early in the ninth century in China. Kanzan was a fine poet-hermit who dwelt near the temple where Jittoku used to live and work. Kanzan would often come out of his hermitage and read his compositions to Jittoku who would heartily appreciate them. Kanzan holds a scroll containing his mountain verses in his hands, while the broom belongs to Jittoku.

坐禪して人か佛になるならハ　厓

40. The Meditating Frog

If a man becomes a Buddha by practising *zazen* . . .
[a frog though I am, I should have been one long ago].

Zazen means 'sitting in meditation'. The frog seems always to be in this posture when we find him in the garden. If the meditation posture alone constitutes Zen, the frog's attainment of Buddhahood is an assured event. But Zen is not mere sitting. There must be an awakening in the Unconscious or Mind. This awakening is called *satori*, or it may be defined as 'innocent knowledge' in Christian terms.

Chih-ch'êng was an avid devotee of meditation before becoming a disciple of Hui-nêng the Sixth Patriarch (d. 713). He spent long hours during the day and throughout the night in this posture. Hui-nêng, seeing this, warned him of the uselessness of 'long sitting' alone. Zen did not consist, he said, of quietly meditating on the Mind; this could become a disease, and is not the way to awaken the *prajñā*, transcendental knowledge:

> When a man is born, he sits;
> When he is dead, he lies.
> O this ill-smelling mass of bones!
> Sitting or lying —
> What is it to you?
> The body comes and goes,
> The Original Nature remains forever the same.

41. Tai-ki and his Lute

What is Tai-ki doing?
Smashing his lute.

戴達何スルカ　コトワリ〜

Tai-ki (Tai-k'uei or Tai An-tao) lived in China in the latter half of the fourth century, and was noted for his scholarly learning and artistic accomplishments. He was especially known for playing the lute. The king wished to have him as one of the court musicians, and sent a messenger to so invite him. But he refused the invitation saying that his art was not meant to amuse the royalty. He is said to have smashed his instrument before the royal messenger. The invitation was later renewed but he persisted in disobeying the order.

In the two lines above there is a pun. A lute is *koto*, and *wari* is breaking, and *kotowari* as a single word means naturally, or rightly, or properly, or as it should be. The idea is that the musician's breaking his favourite instrument was quite justifiable, though apparently lunatic, because he could not stand any insult inflicted upon his genius, which was not to be utilized to entertain a whimsical royal person. Tai-ki was right to be proud of a talent devoted to a spiritual value which was not to be desecrated by 'the world's coarse thumb'.

96

42. Kyōgen Sweeping the Ground

One strike made him forget his
　　learning.
What kind of sound was it?
A piece of brick immediately
　　turned itself into gold.

Zen monk Kyōgen (Hsiang-yen) of China was a disciple of Isan (Wei-shan, 771–853). He was fond of keeping notes of his master's sayings and also extracts from the scriptures, and thought a great deal of them. One day, he found out that all the notes and knowledge he had accumulated were after all of no use in really understanding Zen. He then burned them, and being so disappointed at his inability to gain insight into Reality (*satori*), he decided not to go on any longer with this pursuit. He returned to a country temple where he devoted himself to looking after an old master's grave-yard. One day, while sweeping the ground, it happened that a piece of stone swept away by his broom struck a bamboo nearby. The sound thus produced awakened his mind to a state of enlightenment. He composed a poem in which this 'one strike' is referred to.

Sengai now asks: 'What kind of sound was it that made Kyōgen come to a realization?' He answers in the last two lines.

97

一山門境致　二後人標榜
第三作麼生　放汝六十杖
　　扶桑最初禅窟　梵仙厓拝画

43. Rinzai and the Pine Trees

The first is to beautify the monastery grounds,
The second is to leave a lesson for posterity
   [to learn],
What is the third?
[You have been saved] from sixty blows of my stick.

This refers to Rinzai's dialogue with his teacher Ōbaku (Huang-po, d. 850) when Rinzai (Lin-chi, d. 866) was planting pine trees. Ōbaku said, 'What is the use of planting pines in this remote mountain far away from the village?' Rinzai answered, 'First, for beautifying the monastery grounds; secondly, to bequeath a lesson for the sake of posterity.' So saying, Rinzai struck the earth three times with his spade. Ōbaku returned, 'In spite of all this, you have already had thirty blows of my stick.' Rinzai again tapped the ground thrice with the tip of the spade and drew a long breath. Said Ōbaku, 'Our school will [surely] enjoy much prosperity with you.'

猫乎虎乎
将和唐内乎

是何日龍
人大笑吾亦大咲

44. Tiger and Dragon

(*Left*)   A cat?
           A tiger?
           Or, Watōnai?

(*Right*)   What is this?
           Call it a dragon,
           People laugh heartily,
           And I join them.

Watōnai is a character that comes out prominently in a drama by the famous Japanese playwright Chikamatsu Monzaemon (1653–1724). Once in China with a party of soldiers hunting tigers, Watōnai, instead of killing, tamed the tiger and is thus frequently associated with this animal.

The tiger and the dragon are both symbols of power and energy. The dragon stands also for imperial dignity and is a sign of fortune. In this capacity the dragon is frequently accompanied by the phoenix, as when they speak of the dragon flying and the phoenix dancing. Generally, however, the dragon is associated with the clouds, and the tiger with the bamboo grove. 'The dragon's walk and the tiger's steps' means the display of power and authority.

猫ニ似タモノ

45. The Tiger

Something resembling a cat

It is likely that Sengai never saw a tiger except in paintings, since the tiger is not indigenous to Japan. Sengai could do no better than to follow the general traditional understanding that the animal resembles a cat.

46. The Three
Laughing Sages
at Kokei

なに咲ふ契りわぬ雲和朝夕に
越ゆるもやすし谷の岩橋

Why do they laugh?
The clouds that make no pledges
Pass over the mountain bridge,
Morning or evening,
With the utmost freedom!

The three merry sages here are Eon (Hui-yüan, 332–417), a great Buddhist who was the first to proclaim the teaching of the Pure Land School in China, Tō Emmei (Tao Yüan-ming, 365–427), a Confucian scholar and poet, and Riku Shūsei (Lu Hsiu-ching, 406–477), a Taoist.

The legend goes thus: It so happened that Eon the Buddhist was in the habit of seeing his guests off down the mountain path up to the bridge of Kokei (Hu-ch'i), the Tiger Creek, and no further. One day, the Confucian and the Taoist paid him a call at his temple, Tōrinji (Tung-lin-ssŭ). And as usual Eon came down the mountain with them, but he was enjoying their company so much that he was about to forget his pledge when a tiger roared in time to warn him. They all burst into hearty laughter.

Sengai here contrasts Eon's self-imposed rule with the clouds which, free from all restrictions, human or otherwise, leisurely drift hither and thither, morning or night.

47. The Tiger

A roar —
And the raging wind.

一嘯風烈　　厓

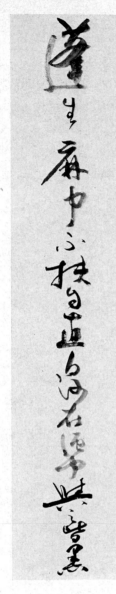

蓬生麻中
不扶自直
白沙在泥中
與之皆黑

老虎出南山

48. Bamboo

(*Left*) The wormwood growing
   among hemp straightens
   up of its own accord;
   The white sand in the muddy
   bog takes on the dark
   colour of the rest.

(*Right*) The old tiger coming out
   from Mt. Nan-shan.

When the old tiger comes out from the southern mountain he brings the wind with him. The bamboos indicate his proximity.

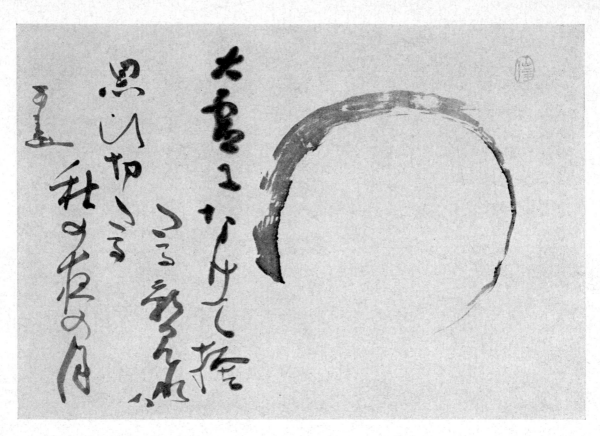

大虚になけて拾たる影見れハ
思い切たる秋の夜の月　　厓

49. The Moon

When I see [Reality's] shadow
Thrown into the emptiness of space,
How boldly defined
The moon
Of the autumnal night!

When the ego is thrown out into the vacuity of nothingness, or better, when the ego is identified with the absolute Emptiness (*śūnyatā*), how free, how unimpededly expanded one feels! The autumnal moon symbolizes the state of mind one then realizes. It is 'the moon of suchness' that Buddhist poets talk so much about, and Sengai tried to picture it for us.

The Japanese word for bold is *omoi kittaru*, which is graphic, vital and dynamic. *Omoi* is thought, thinking, deliberation, hesitancy, etc. *Kiru*, the root of *kittaru*, means to cut. *Omoi kittaru*, therefore, is throwing away all deliberation radically, with no fear of the consequences. The participial phrase here used is a strong expression applied to an act unqualifiedly or even desperately carried out. By using it in reference to the autumnal moon whose whole being is clarity itself ungrudgingly presented in its uttermost fullness to our view, Sengai gives vent to his own state of mind, which, the Chinese say, is 'in its eight phases (or facets), transparent through and through'.

50. The Monkeys and the Moon

To what shall this life of ours be compared?
It's like the monkey trying to reach out [at the
    moon reflected in the water]:
When one arm is stretched out,
The other is to be pulled back.
[Thus the law of relativity rules our life here on
    earth. You cannot have everything as your
    greedy mind desires and contrives.]

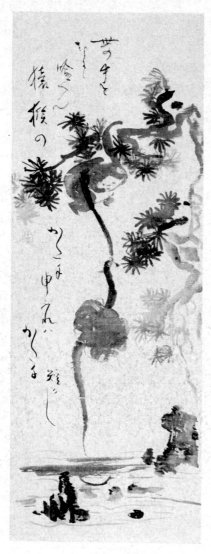

世の中をなにゝ喩へん猿猴の
かた手申ふれハかた手短かし

This picture is generally understood as depicting the monkey's stupidity in trying to catch the reflected moon in the water, but Sengai gives his own interpretation.

51. Illusion   目を推せハ二ツ出て来る秋の月

Press the eyeballs
And lo!
Two autumnal moons.

A slight pressure of the finger on the eyeball makes us see double. The autumn moon, flawless in its illumination, represents the Moon of Suchness or Reality itself. Yet, however clear and bright the Moon, if there is an obstruction it will take on a false appearance.

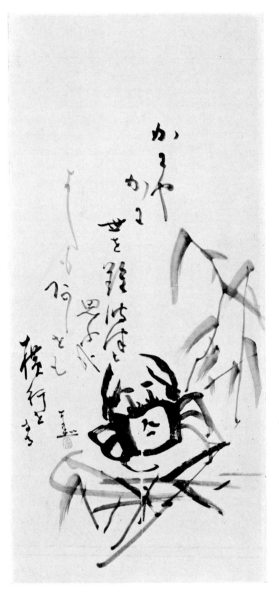

かにやかに世を難波津と思ふ哉
よしも阿しをも横行する　厓

O crab, O crab!
You seem to think the world is
　　like the marshland of Naniwa.
You walk freely over the reeds [good
　　and evil].

Reeds are called *yoshi* in some localities and in others *ashi*. *Yoshi* means good, and *ashi* bad, though this moral valuation has nothing to do with the name of the plant itself. Sengai makes use of this double meaning of the words. He compares this world where good and evil are inseparably intermingled to the marshland of reeds of *yoshi* and *ashi*. The crab is likened to a wise man of enlightenment whose eyes while in this world are opened to a transcendental realm of absolute Good.

Naniwa refers to the ancient site of the city of Osaka, while the ideograms may also read 'this difficult world' or 'this world of vicissitudes'.[1]

_____
[1] Compare Nos. 53, 54.

53. The Skull よし阿しハ目口鼻から出るものか

Good and bad
Do they come out
Of the eyes, mouth, and nose?

Modern Buddhist thinkers would say not only out of the five senses but also out of the intellect (*manovijñāna*). I do not know why we are given just five senses and no more or less. Had we six or seven or eight, the world as we now have it would be quite a different field of experience. The chief advantage, as well as disadvantage, with the intellect is that it discriminates and will not go any further than that. That is to say, it just discriminates and stops there; it does not go beyond itself nor does it sink into itself. It depends on the senses for its operation and thinks that there is nothing beyond or beneath the senses. It thus fails to recognize the real value of life, which makes use of the senses and is not in them. The intellect is the prodigal son who forgot his original home. He is to be told of it and is to come back to it. Where is the original home then? Sengai represents it here as a skull.

Yoshi and *ashi* are puns. They both mean marsh reeds. As explained earlier, in certain districts they are called *yoshi* while in others they are called *ashi* — and *yoshi* also means good, *ashi* bad. *Yoshi* and *ashi* thus refer to the same plant that shoots out of the skull, and yet when two people of different localities see them they contradict each other as far as names are concerned. Our moral evaluation is, in a sense, a matter of nomenclature conditioned by time and space as discriminated by the intellect. The problem of sin comes up when naming or knowledge takes its rise and Eden is lost. In Eden there is no question of good and evil; everything we did or saw was good. Knowledge discriminates, and discrimination is sin. What we need now is innocent knowledge, that is, knowledge that does not know itself — knowledge that transcends itself.

Sengai's skull, then, is the original home out of which the plant, sometimes called good (*yoshi*) and sometimes bad (*ashi*), shoots forth rampantly. When the intellect and the senses are not warned of their promiscuous operation, the skull will burst to their own ruination.

The skull reminds one of Chuang-tzu's allegory of Chaos (*konton*). The gods, who had just finished creating a new world, thought: 'We owe a great deal to our friend Chaos without whose silent and self-effacing help we could not have accomplished our task. Let us repay him and show our gratitude for his invaluable co-operation.' After much deliberation they decided, in return for his favour, to give Chaos all the senses they themselves were enjoying. One after another they supplied Chaos with the senses, and finally the work was completed. As they were congratulating themselves on the splendid consummation, Chaos died.

When good and evil were differentiated, the world of knowledge started; or, when knowledge began to operate, the world of good and evil came to be differentiated. Either way will do. While in Eden, where innocence prevailed, we did not know where we were; indeed, we were non-existent. Now we know, which means Eden is no more with us, and we long for it. The question is: Will we ever regain that paradise lost? Sengai elsewhere instructs us:

> Just because [we are]
> In the midst of good and evil
> This cool evening breeze![1]

The privilege of being human is to discriminate good from evil, and just because of this discrimination we can transcend the two and live in a world of innocence.

[1] Compare Nos. 52, 54 and 55.

I must repeat myself, and say that the transcendence does not mean dropping off, or leaving behind, or ignoring, or being indifferent, and that 'the cool evening breeze' cannot be enjoyed in the void. Eden and the Saha[1] world are coexistent. Paradise is not something to 'regain' but to recognize.

[1] The finite world of endurance and patience.

よし阿しの中を流れて清水哉

54. Reeds

Amidst the reeds [good and evil]
Runs
The pure spring water.

As reeds are known in some districts as *yoshi* (good) and in other districts as *ashi* (evil), 'Amidst the reeds' therefore means 'where good and evil are confusingly asserted' — that is, this human world of ours. 'The pure spring water' is the enlightened man who is tainted neither by good nor by evil.[1]

[1] Compare Nos. 52, 53 and 55.

55. Amidst Reeds

Just because of our being in the midst of
   good and evil (reeds),[1]
This cool evening breeze is enjoyed.

[1] Compare Nos. 52, 53 and 54.

よし阿しの中にこそ阿れ
夕納涼　　　厓

生かそふと　ころそふと　　崖

56. The Spoon

Whether for life, whether for death,
[Depends upon this doctor's spoonful.]

切れ縄に口ちハなけれと朧月　厓

57. The Realistic Rope

A dim, moonlit night,
Broken pieces of rope,
Though mouthless!

Buddhists often use this simile to illustrate the effect of illusory thoughts. In the semi-darkness pieces of rope may take on an image of snakes — though mouthless.

Buddhist philosophers distinguish three forms of knowledge: Illusory Knowledge, Relative Knowledge, and Absolute or Perfect Knowledge. The last form of knowledge is *prajñā*, and has been variously described and referred to as transcendental wisdom, original knowledge, primary knowledge which cannot be taught or gained from a teacher.

117

58. The Puppy

'Kyan, kyan!'

きやん～　厓

The puppy is yelping. He is tied to a stick and does not like it. He wants to be free of anything extra attached to him which is foreign to his nature. Sengai is amused to see most of his fellow beings symbolized in this innocent creature. Strangely, we like to put on ourselves things we really do not require and because of those superfluities we drive ourselves into the tight corner, and cry out for a rescue. Instead of being master of those extraneous attachments, we enslave ourselves to them. When Sengai drew this small dog, he must have been meditating on human follies.

118

堪 忍
堪忍のなるかんにんかかん忍か
ならぬ堪忍す流かかん忍　　匡

59.

Patience:
    It is no patience which you can bear
      patiently;
    Patience is to bear what is unbearable.

This is a proverbial saying, which Sengai composed into a rhythmic thirty-one syllable poem.

仰而観天　伏而察地
有物如珠　一而不二
　　　　崖

60. Mount Fuji

Looking up, the heavens are seen extending;
Looking down, the earth is seen stretched,
Both to the farthest ends of the horizon!
Beyond, there shines a white pearl,
The only one, and no second!

はへの風　世の中ハ皆　間切舟　厓

61. Sailing Boats

When the winds from the south prevail,
All things in the world move along like
　　sailing boats.

South wind means smooth sailing, while north and east winds indicate rough
waters.

戰々兢々　人過於橋上
如何　橋流而水不流

62. A Man Crossing a Log-Bridge

Fu Daishi (Fu-ta-shih, 497–569) wrote the following famous Zen verse:

> A man holds a spade empty-handedly,
> He walks on foot while riding on a water-buffalo.
> He passes over a bridge;
> The bridge flows and the water does not.

Sengai referring to this verse playfully writes:

> Trembling, shaking,
> A man passes over the bridge.
> How is [the statement] that the bridge flows
> And the water does not?

Fu Daishi was one of those Zen sages who did not fall into the orthodox line of transmission. Legend makes him a contemporary of Bodhidharma and has both coming from the Tushita Heaven, where Maitreya is waiting for his turn to appear in the human world when the present Badra kalpa comes to an end. Fu's life as is recorded in the *Dentōroku* (*The Transmission of the Lamp*, fas. 27) is full of miracles. He is, however, quite an earthly being as he is reportedly the inventor of the revolving book case, known as *rinzō*, which literally means 'the tripitaka on a wheel'.

63. Onoe Shinshichi

'Ladies and Gentlemen. I am Onoe Shinshichi, an actor recently arriving from Edo. I am going to present to you a play called "Seven Transformations", which every actor plays once in his life.

'Attention, please. There are six paths of existence: hell, hungry ghosts, animal life, the fighting devils, the human world, and the celestial kingdom. If these six performances are successfully done, to the best of my ability, may I attain Buddhahood!

'Ladies and Gentlemen. This is my farewell performance, and I wish you to allow me first to play life in hell.

'Look! look! Here comes the *oni* (demon). [The picture depicts the scene.] Thank you very much, Ladies and Gentlemen. *Namu-amida-butsu, namu-amida-butsu.*'

The motive of the play is to demonstrate that it is the mind that assumes all these six or seven forms of existence, that all is mind-made. The character 'mind' (*kokoro*) is distinctly written on the apron of the actor. The name of the actor is Onoe Shinshichi. The first is the family name of a famous line of actors. But the second is probably Sengai's invention, where *shin* is mind and *shichi* means seven, or mind in its seven transformations. Edo is what Tokyo was called in feudal times, but Sengai has cleverly replaced the two characters for Edo by two others which are also read *edo*, meaning, this defiled world.

尾上心七
東西〜新下り穢土役者尾上心七
一世一代なゝはけの狂言アレアレ
最初地獄より餓鬼畜生修羅人間天上
む通りの所作事首尾よふ御目に
留りますれハ佛とはけるか
総方様への御暇乞ひ先ツハ地獄
鬼志や〜よふ〜難有
南無阿彌陀佛〜

[Drawing 63]

64. Bamboos

For whom,
     this cool refreshing breeze?

The worldly pictures are like a pretty
    woman who hates being laughed at
    by others;
But my drawings are like a comedian
    who loves being laughed at.
Says Lao-tzu, 'When ordinary mortals
    look at me, they ridicule.' This is
    proof
[that he is not one of them.]

爲誰起清風
  世画如美女憎爲人所笑
  厓画如戯者愛爲人所笑
  老子曰下愚見之大笑可以見已

二見浦一目に見れハ不二の雪

65. The Bay of Futami
(Futami-ga-ura)

This seventeen syllable poem or haiku on Futami-ga-ura is difficult to translate.

> The Bay of Futami
> With one eye seen,
> Snow on Mount Fuji.

Futami-ga-ura, literally two sight-Bay, is in the province of Ise near the famous Ise Shintō Shrine. The Bay is named after the huge rocks rising off-shore above the waters. One is larger than the other. They symbolize conjugal love, and the sacred rope, therefore, ties them together.

The poem was probably composed one fine New Year's Day when not a cloud obstructed the view. The rocks were seen clearly coming out of the waves as was, at the same time, Mount Fuji, capped with snow and rising magnificently in the far distance. The Futami rocks thus seen in combination with Mount Fuji,

126

which symbolizes immaculate beauty, are most auspicious signs for the year just ushered in. With 'one eye' seen, means that these two symbols of good luck are caught at one glance; that is, luck is doubled.

The haiku, besides this apparent interpretation, permits of an esoteric one. *Futami*, two objects of vision, stands for two, and *hitome*, one eye, for one. *Fuji*, though originally meaning fire in Ainu, can be written in two ways in Sino-Japanese characters, one meaning wealthy gentleman, and the other meaning not-two. Sengai uses the latter. Both may be read *fuji*. Thus we have here a haiku composed of numbers, two (rocks), one (glance), not-two (Fuji).

These three figures, in this order, are singularly significant, as they show us the way Buddhist philosophers have come to view the world and life. Generally, we begin with some sort of dualism, and arrive at monism, and stop there. But the Buddhist position goes further. In 'The Inscription on the Believing Mind' by Sōsan (Sêng-ts'an, d. 606), the Third Patriarch of Zen Buddhism in China, we find: 'Two is possible because of the one, but do not stop at the one.' How then can we go further? There is, Buddhists would say, another position known as advaitism, that is, non-dualism or a-dualism, or not-two. Sengai makes full use of the coincidence he saw in the two ways of representing the name of Japan's most celebrated mountain.

Advaitism is not negativistic, as it might superficially seem. It is to be understood positively. The main point is not to be partial to any determinable school of thought. When Buddhists say not-two, they also mean not-one, not-three, not-many, not absolute, and so on. Naturally, some may say, we cannot live on sheer negation, there must be something positive. If it is not this, it must be that. We need something nameable, positively determinable. We must have 'it'. The Buddhist answer is: The objection is all right as far as it goes, but it must not be forgotten that a denial always implies an affirmation within itself and that we cannot go on forever denying. To go on denying and not to know where to stop is nonsense. Where then must we stop? Buddhists would say, stop where you cannot stop. When you realize that stopping is a not-stopping, you know where to stop. Let us therefore go on denying and still denying, until the time comes upon us when we feel that we cannot continue like this and that we must willy-nilly make a big bundle of all the denials we have been amassing and throw them overboard into the ocean of infinity, whatever that may be. Then for the first time we realize that the ultimate something or 'it' we have been looking for has been with us ever since we made the first denial, for the first denial is no other than

127

the ultimate affirmation. Hence the Buddhist philosophy of advaitism, which is the philosophy of isness, or as-it-is-ness.

Zen, being a form of Buddhism which developed in China, shares the view presented here. But Zen is not a philosophy and has its own way of demonstrating the point. For instance, the master may produce a stick and say, 'Do not call this a stick, nor call it a not-stick. What do you call it?' Or sometimes he will tell you, 'The willow is green, and the flower is red,' but at times he will contradict himself and say, 'The willow is not green, and the flower is not red.' His logic does not stop here, for he will go on, 'And therefore the willow is a willow and the flower a flower.'

I said at the beginning that Sengai's haiku may be interpreted esoterically, but this is misleading because we have seen that there is nothing esoteric about it. In fact, Zen is far from being esoteric or being anything specific. Some say that Zen is mystical or secretive, or obscurantist, or purposely misleading, but you will find they are all wrong.

Whether Sengai composed this haiku with the above points in mind I cannot tell. But I would like to read in it all these thoughts which I have been able only briefly to describe. Indeed, all his works, literary or otherwise, are to be interpreted with these thoughts in mind. It would be committing a gross mistake to consider him as merely a common cartoonist or humorist for popular amusement. He is a serious teacher of Zen.

函浦晚望

山々繞海望中重　七里清灘十里松
華表千年鶴何在　仙宮無恙夕陽鐘
　　　　　　　　　厓

66. The Evening View of Hakoura Beach

Mountain after mountain,
Surrounding the sea far away to the horizon,
The beach extends as far as the eyes can survey;
And a range of pine trees seems to run on even further.
The torii gate one thousand years ago,
Where is the sacred crane?
The heavenly shrine stands quiet and peaceful,
And the evening bell booms out sonorously.

世の中を何に喩へん電の
露の命と思ふ間もなし　厓　　　　67. Lightning

To what shall I compare this life of ours?
Even before I can say it is like a flash of
lightning or a dew-drop, it is no more.

The *Diamond Sūtra* (*Vajracchedīkā-prajñāpāramitā-sūtra*) has likened life to six evanescent phenomena we see around us: a dream, a vision, a bubble, a shadow, a flash of lightning, and a dew drop. The idea of transiency must have deeply affected the Buddhist mind in India. 'All things are impermanent; all is subject to constant becoming' — this is the theme Buddhists are never tired of harping on. But fortunately they have never forgotten the fact that the idea of impermanency is always lined by that of permanency. The two ideas go hand in hand, though verbally they are sharply defined as contrasting or contradicting. They would thus say: A is A because A is not-A. What is needed of us, who are ever seeking for a life immortal, is to recognize the truth that aspiration is realization, and that this truth is not recognizable by logic but by actual experience.

危崖千尺攀蘿而過
右翻芭蕉之句　崖道人

68. The Kiso Gorge

The cliffs towering dangerously high,
People pass by, clinging to the vines.
　　　　　The picture is after Bashō's poem.

In his *Diary of Travel Through Sarashina*, Bashō has:

The hanging bridge,
Our lives entwined
By the ivy vines.
(*Trans. R. H. Blyth*)

131

69. Infirmities of Old Age

Wrinkles on the face, dark spots grow on the skin, and the back bent;
Bald-headed and grey-bearded,
The hands tremble, the legs totter, and gone are the teeth,
Hard of hearing and eyesight bedimmed.
Indispensable are a hood on the head, wrappers, a stick, and spectacles;
Then a hot-water bottle, a heating stone, a chamber pot, and a back-
    scratcher.
Meddlesome he is, afraid of dying, and lonesome;
Suspicious of others, the desire for possession grows stronger.
Repetitive, short-tempered, and querulous;
Obtrusive and officious.
The same stories over again and again in which his own children are
    invariably praised.
Boastful of his health, he makes others feel tired beyond endurance.

Old Sayings

志わかよ流ほ黒か出ける腰曲る
頭まかはけるひけ白くな流
手は賑ふ足ハよろつく歯は抜る
耳はきこへす目ハうとくなる
身に添は頭巾襟巻杖目鏡
たんぽおん志やく志ゆひん孫子手
聞たかる死とむなかる淋しかる
心ハ曲る欲深ふなる
くとくなる気短になる愚ちになる
出志やはりたか流世話やきたかる
又しても同し咄しに子を誉る
達者自まんに人はいやかる
　古人の哥　　　　　厓書

[Drawing 69]

70. An Old Man's Excuse

If you say, 'Come later!'
They will soon be back to carry you off.
Better tell them, 'Not at home till I'm 99'.

後と云へは又も向いに来流へし
九十九迄ハ留すとこたへろ

　This is an old man's attempt to outwit the messenger of death. Merely to say 'Come later', will not assure us a long enough life. He hopes to cheat King Yama's devils by feigning absence for a very long time to come. Let us hope the devils may be beguiled.

133

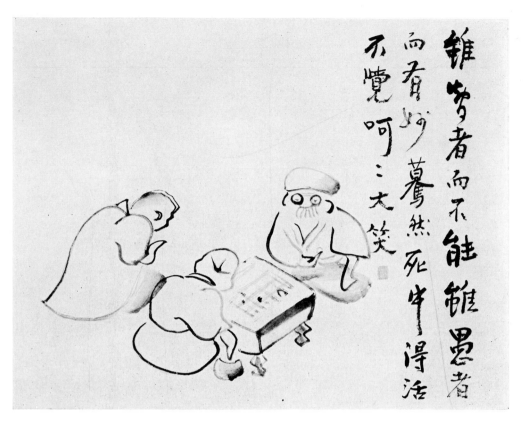

雖智者而不能雖愚者而有妙
驀然死中得活不覺呵々大笑　　　71. The *Go* Players

There are things that even the wise fail to do, while the fool hits the
point. Unexpectedly discovering the way to life in the midst of death,
he burst out in hearty laughter!

A *go* game, like chess, requires much imagination and ingenious calculation.
It is a game very much indulged-in in Japan among the cultured and leisured class
of people. Sengai was known to have been a pretty shrewd player. In playing this
game, the player is frequently put into a corner where if he misses a move all is
lost. Such a player would then often spend as long as several hours, or even days,
to find the way out of the dilemma. When this is found he arises alive from out of
the midst of 'death'. This is 'Man's extremity is God's opportunity' in our daily
life. In the study of Zen we too experience this. Hence Sengai's reference here.

右や左りのお旦那様

72. A Crippled Beggar

Honourable Gentlemen to my left and to my right . . .

It is interesting to note that Sengai often chose to draw subjects which were generally connected with the lower side of social life. They were taken from events in the lives of the common folk. A monk though he was, he showed a great interest in the world around him and befriended, regardless of their profession, people of all kinds. We must bear in mind that in feudal days the head priests of temples patronized by the ruling class of the time moved among the chosen company of the day. Sengai never forgot to mix with the masses.

135

此味噌漬ハ怡土志摩大一の名物
上けてくれなんせ　　　崖

73. A Woman Offering Pickles

These *miso* pickles are the best-known products of Itoshima. Be good enough to accept them [O Reverend Master].

The woman is apparently from the gay quarters near Itoshima ward, showing that the retired abbot of Shōfukuji befriended those living there. His loving, congenial spirit penetrated every walk of human life and made him approachable by everybody.

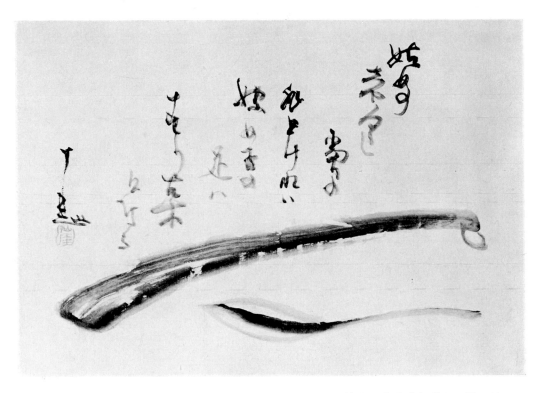

姑めの志やくし當りの飛とけれハ
嫁め子の足ハすり古木となる　崖

74. The Ladle and the Pestle

When the mother-in-law's ladle is too severely in use,
The daughter-in-law's legs become stiff like [a pair of]
    pestles.

The mother-in-law is proverbially hard on her son's wife, one who is newly adopted into the family. The latter is mercilessly ordered about too frequently and too severely by the matron of her new home. Trying to carry out her orders, the young wife has to do much moving from one place to another, and finally her legs give out, they turn into a stiff pair of sticks, like a big wooden pestle used in the kitchen. This is a warning to the mother-in-law not to be unreasonably severe to her newly-adopted daughter.

國以民為基　人以農為命

75. The Farmers

The state is founded on its people;
And the life of the people depends
on agriculture.

76. The Singing Horse-Driver

On the Hill,
The sun is shining, shining;
While at Suzuka,
It is cloudy.

坂ハ照る〜
鈴鹿ハ曇なー

This is Sengai's own variation of the original folk song which is generally sung by the palanquin carriers along their road which starts from a hill. The original song goes like this:

On the Hill,
The sun is shining, shining;
While at Suzuka,
It is cloudy;
When we come to Ai no Tsuchiyama,
It is rain.

吉野ても花の下より鼻の下　崖

77. The Cherry-Blossoms at Yoshino

A company of women (and wine) is better
　　than the blooming cherries,
Even at Yoshino.

This is a play on the words 'flower' and 'nose' which are both *hana* in Japanese. Thus *hana no shita* may mean 'below the blooming flowers' as well as 'below the nose'. 'Below the nose' is an abbreviation for *hana no shita ga nagai*, meaning that the distance between the nose and the upper lip is long, thought to signify a person who is erotically disposed. Yoshino is full of cherry-blossoms in the spring, and it is crowded with gay parties accompanied by geishas and other entertaining women. (See No. 83.)

册々孤生竹　結根泰山河　　厓

78. Bamboos

Thickly growing bamboos,
    each stand singly;
Put all their roots together,
    and all is well in the mountains and rivers.

夜をこめてとりの

79. The Cock

> The night is advancing
> And the cock . . .

This is the first part of an *uta* or poem by the Japanese authoress Sei Shōnagon. She was a noted court lady of the early eleventh century who proved her literary talent and originality of imagination in her *Makura-no-sōshi* or *The Pillow Book*. The whole verse reads:

> The night is advancing
> And the cock,
> His crowing may be imitated,
> But the frontier gate of love
> Will never permit mockery.

The story of mocking the cock in early morning goes thus: When the Chinese Chou dynasty (1122–255 B.C.) showed signs of decline in the fourth century B.C., it produced what is known as the Period of Warring States. The empire was split into many kingdoms and dukedoms which were constantly engaged in warfare in its various forms. When Mō Shōkun (Mêng Ch'ang Chün of Ch'i) with his followers was kept in a state of captivity in a neighbouring kingdom called Ch'in, he sought to escape. The frontier gate which divided Ch'in from Ch'i was found closed, and the gate-keepers refused to open the gate for the escapees because it was still dark and the cock had not announced the dawn. Mō Shōkun could not wait, the pursuers being close at his heels. Among his followers an expert imitator of a crowing cock then cried out 'cock-a-doodle-doo' to perfection, and the gate was opened.

雪後吐芳　　匡

80.　The Plum-Blossoms

After the snow
The fragrance
All the more.

大原女の柴に苅そふ花の香も
都の春にかわらぬものを

81. The Ōhara Maids

The flowers decorate the kindling wood
The Ōhara maids carry;
The sweet odour of spring
Is auspiciously spread over the miyako (capital).

Ōhara Village is not far from Kyoto, the ancient capital of Japan. The Ōhara women have a special way of carrying on their heads bundles of fuel which they sell to the city dwellers. Flowers picked in the fields decorate these prosaic piles of household goods, bringing the auspicious sign of spring to those in the *miyako*.

82. Bamboos

Bamboo-shoots?
They must be of the Mōsō
    family,
Coming out so early.

Mōsō is a type of bamboo, and the word can also mean already (*mō*) and so (*sō*). Sengai plays on the word and the name, and refers to the bamboo-shoots that are already out so early in the spring.

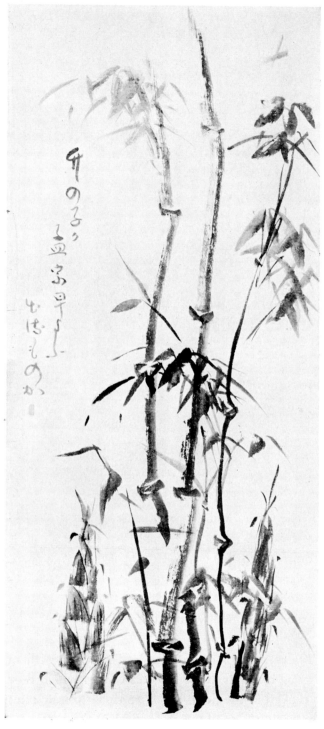

竹の子か孟宗早よふ出流ものか

146

農其天下之本乎
楽しみハ花の下より鼻の下　厓

83. The Farmers

(They say that) there is more pleasure under the nose
　　than under the blossoms.
(But) we farmers are the foundation of the world.

There is a play on the words nose and blossoms which are both pronounced *hana* in Japanese. The expression 'under the nose' or 'a long upper lip' means amorousness, while 'under the flowers or blossoms' refers to the gay parties often held under blossoming cherry trees. Sengai is pointing here to another and a more profound kind of pleasure. (See also No. 77.)

84. Sugawara Michizane

天下梅花主　扶桑文字祖
噫　鎮西太宰府

Sugawara Michizane (845–903) was, in the history of Japan, one of the great scholars of Chinese classical literature during the Heian period. The Emperor Daigo, wishing to crush the politically all-powerful Fujiwara family, appointed Michizane to an important government position which was hereditarily filled by one of the Fujiwaras. But even the Emperor failed to cope with the social and political pressure which ignored the significance of the individual. The Sugawara family ranked lower than the Fujiwara. Later, falsely accused, Michizane was deposed and sent in exile to the Western capital of Dazai-fu in Kyūshū, far removed from the political, social and cultural capital of Kyoto. After three years of a desolate life, he died.

His famous poem, full of pathos, composed while in Dazaifu runs:

> When the east wind blows
> Send your sweet scent,
> O my plum blossoms!
> Though your master is gone,
> Forget not that Spring is here again.

After his death, Michizane was defined as the god of literature, and there is a famous shrine dedicated to him in the northern section of Kyoto known as Tenjin, Heavenly God. The above inscription reads:

> God of the Plum Blossoms in the whole world,
> Lord of Literature in the Land of the Rising Sun.
> Alas!
> Dazaifu, capital of the Western frontier!

148

85. The Cascade of Mt. Rai

The cascade
Falling among the trees,
And the spring breeze
Makes us think of scattering blossoms.

雷山瀧の写意
瀧水の落る木間の春風に
吹ちる花と人や見るらん

149

86. The Plum-Blossoms

The fragrant scent gently
flowing in the dusk,
And the evening moon.

Sengai is quoting the famous couplet on the plum-blossoms by Rin Wasei (Lin Ho-ching) of the Sung dynasty. The preceding line reads:

The leafless branches, inclining,
Reflect themselves across the water,
shallow and clear.

暗香浮動　月黃昏　　崖・

150

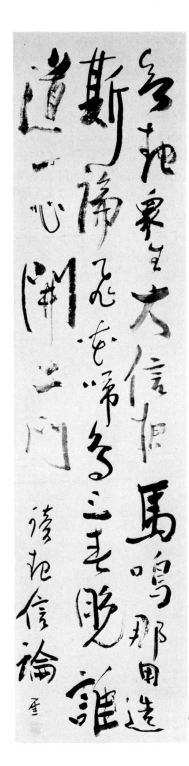

To awaken all beings to absolute faith,
(This is the one thing that is most needed.)
What then is the use of Aśvaghosha writing
       this discourse?

The flowers are being scattered about and
      the birds are singing these
      late spring days.
Who would waste time arguing about the One
      Mind and its Two Aspects?

欲起衆生大信根　馬鳴那用造斯論
飛花啼鳥三春晩　誰道一心開二門
　　　　　　　読起信論　厓

    Aśvaghosha was a great Indian philosopher of Buddhism who probably lived about the beginning of the Christian era. His work on the Awakening of Faith is a fine introduction to Mahāyāna Buddhism. There is One Mind, he says, which has two aspects, Suchness (*tathatā*) and Birth-and-death (*samsāra*). Mind as Suchness corresponds to the Godhead, and the Mind as Birth-and-death to God the creator. The one is static — just is, or just given — while the other is dynamic — subject to birth and death, ever becoming. But, 'what is', is not to be sought outside of 'what becomes'. Being is becoming and becoming is being. Zen is to understand this concretely through one's personal experience.

    This concrete experience individually actualized is basic; thought and language start from it. This basic experience, *satori*, cannot be expressed in language, because as soon as it is so expressed it becomes abstract, conceptualized and removed from life itself; it thus becomes a common property on sale in the open market.

If, however, this experience is to be expressed in words, they must be selected with particular care, so that their meaning in the context is not confused with their ordinary meaning; that is to say, the words should express not knowledge but that faith which is called 'great' or 'absolute'. This is where the great battle takes place between knowledge and faith, science and religion, fact and fiction, history and mythology, rationalities and absurdities. The Zen master also participates in the heated contest, but knows at the same time how to cool himself 'in the summer evening breeze in the midst of good and evil', as Sengai says elsewhere. Hence, 'the flowers are being scattered about and the birds are singing these late spring days.'

88. The Toad

呑てくれよふ〜と
出掛たり　　厓

Gobble-you-up,
Gobble-you-up,
Advances the toad.

One of the most interesting sights during the rainy season is that of a toad making his way somewhere. He crawls along with such composure and gravity; with Great Wisdom, one might say.

153

89. The Morning-glory

The dawning day dies
   Like the know-nothing crystal dew.
Does it bloom with real life,
   The morning-glory?
         (Trans. by R. H. Blyth)

A flowering morning-glory entwines a bamboo fence. The thirty-one syllable verse celebrates the morning-glory, which blossoms beautifully in the morning and withers helplessly in the evening.

明る日ハ暮るものとも志ら露を
命に咲か　阿さ顔の花

154

90. Lotus

However muddy the water is, the lotus retains its purity; indeed it blooms beautifully just because it grows out of the mud.

The clear drops shed on my
    sleeves
Are the dew drops on the
    lotus leaves of the
    Buddha-body.

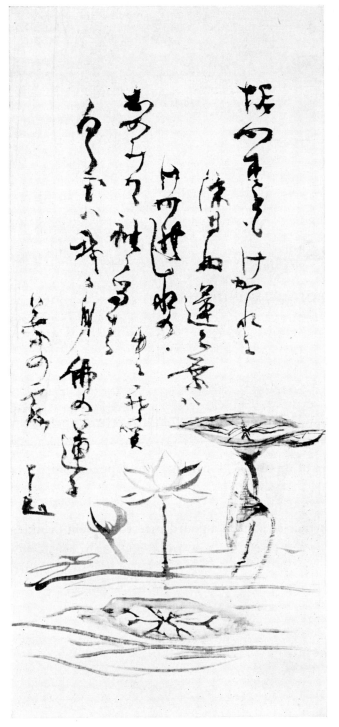

垢かすともけかれに染まぬ蓮子葉ハ
けか禮し水の中にこそ咲
おかみつ、袖に留まる白玉ハ
我が身佛の蓮子葉の露　　　　厓

155

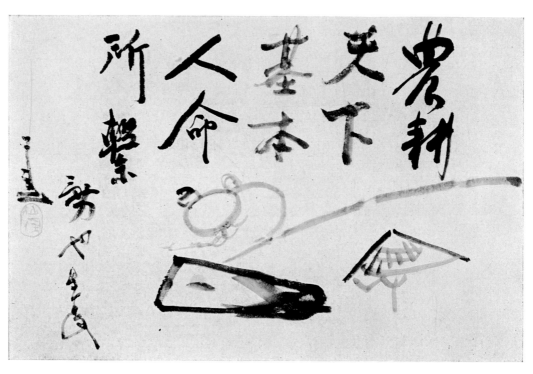

農耕天下基本人命所繋
務や生民　　厓

91. Farmers

Farming is the foundation of the world, for human life depends on it.
So strive on [O you, people]!

The picture shows a hoe, a farmer's hat, and a gourd used to contain drinking water.

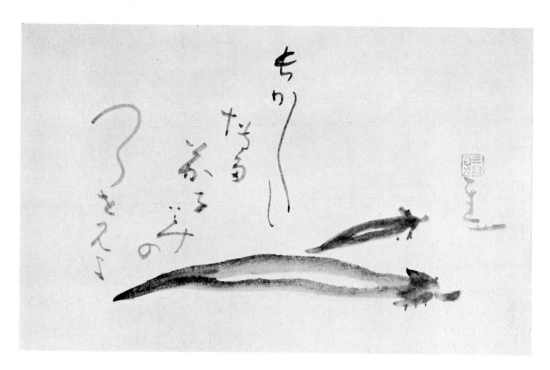

長か～し博多茄子美の
つらを見よ　　匡

92. Eggplants

Look at the long, long faces of the eggplants
grown in Hakata. [How long and glossy!]

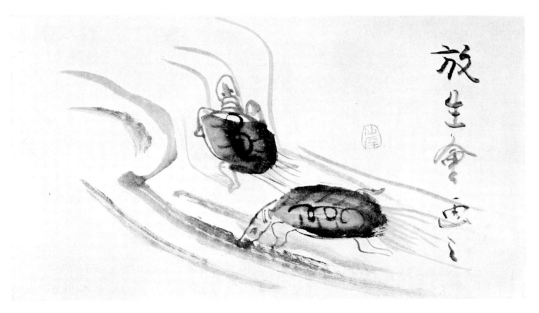

放生會画之

93. Animal or Life Preservation Day

In Buddhism, one day a year is set aside for 'releasing [and giving] life' by preventing the destruction of living creatures. Human beings are largely dependent on other living things such as fish, animals and vegetables for their existence. To remember how much we are indebted to them and to express our grateful feeling, fish and birds (or tortoises, as are here depicted) are freed to return to nature accompanied by the chanting of sūtras.

94. Kensu the Beggar

Not to kill is the precept,
To release the living from [confinement
   is charity].

戒殺放生

159

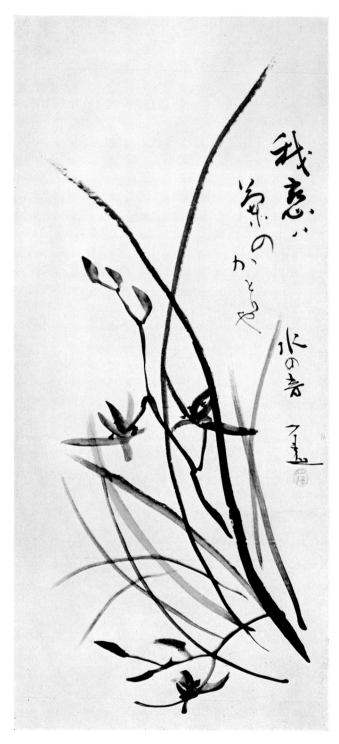

我恋ハ蘭のかをりや水の音　厓

95. The Orchids

My love is
The fragrance of the orchid
And the sound of water.

What 'sound of water' Sengai likes to hear is not clear. Perhaps he refers to Bashō's famous haiku on the sound of water made by the frog jumping into the old pond. (See No. 110.)

As to the orchid's fragrance, this brings to mind the encounter between a Confucian poet and a Zen master. The poet came to the Zen master one day and asked, 'What is Tao (Way)?' The master said, 'Your teacher has a fine saying in his *Analect*. Tao is given in it.' 'To what do you refer?' asked the poet. 'It goes, I have nothing to hide from you. Tao is everywhere. If you have eyes you can see it,' was the master's response. The poet failed to grasp the meaning. Later, as they went walking in the mountain the wild laurel were seen in full bloom. The master pointed at the trees and asked, 'Do you smell the fragrant laurel?' 'Yes, I do, Master,' replied the poet. 'There! I have nothing to hide from you. Herein you enter.'

秋風に染井の岡の紅葉は
怡土志摩かけて錦なりけ利

96. The Somei Hill

As the autumn winds begin to blow,
The leaves on Somei Hill are turning crimson
A way to Ito Isle,
Weaving variegated sheets of brocade.

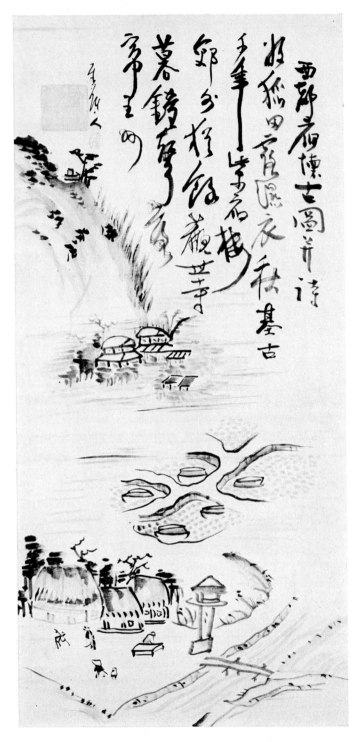

97. The Western Capital

Rice fields are all over
Where once stood the imposing edifices of the Western Capital.
It's autumn now and the farmers are busy with harvesting.
My sleeves are wet with dew (tears).
What is left of the olden days of a thousand years ago?
Is the lone temple dedicated to Avalokiteśvara, God of Mercy?
The evening bell sends out its resonance all over the sites once of the Imperial residence.

[See No. 84]

西都府懐古図并詩

収稲田露湿衣秋　基古千年紫府樓
郊外猶餘観世寺　暮鐘聲落帝王州
　　　　　　　　　　　厓陳人

そしるなよ
庭の阿たりに
菊の花　　厓

98. Chrysanthemum

Don't slight,
There is a chrysanthemum
Somewhere in the yard.

What Sengai probably means here is that we should not think lightly of his little hut for, however humble it may appear, somewhere in the yard there is a blooming chrysanthemum which is incomparable in its unworldly beauty.

One bright moon of mid-autumn illuminates
    the whole world.

    In Japan as well as in China the moon shines brightest
on the night of the fifteenth day of the ninth month
according to the lunar calendar. The mid-autumn sky is
clear with no vapour. It is then a full moon and the
moon goddess is celebrated with offerings of rice dump-
lings, wild autumnal flowers, and a jar of saké.

一輪明月掛中秋

100. My Mountain Hut

In a mountain hut
Living alone this autumn eve,
The call of the wild pigeon
Seems almost to say:
Dō dō shitakai, *dō shitakai* (How are you faring?)

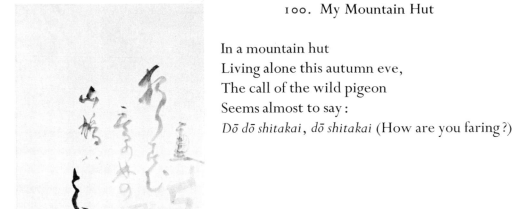

獨りすむ庵の林の山鳩ハ
とふ〜志たかひ
とふしたかひとこそ
きけはき、野流
秋の夕くれ　　　　崖

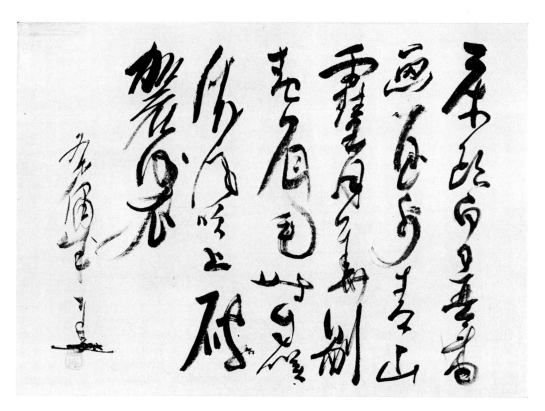

床頭白日琴書画　屋外青山霎月華
剔起眉毛時自咲　清風吹上破袈裟
右偶成　匡

101. My Tattered Surplice

'In the sun on my porch, I look at pictures and writings;
Outside, the green mountains, the snow, the moon,
and cherry flowers.
I lift my head, and smile to myself;
The pure wind blows my tattered surplice.'
(*Trans. by R. H. Blyth*)

大日如来眞言を以て
人界の春るを加持志奉る
阿まてらす國を清よめて初烏

102. The New Year

By means of the Mantram of the Great Illuminating
Buddha, I pray for the auspicious ushering-in of the
coming year on this earth of human habitation: The
first cry of the crow!
May this country of ours be kept purified
Where shineth the heavenly sun.
[The crow is a symbol of the sun.]

168

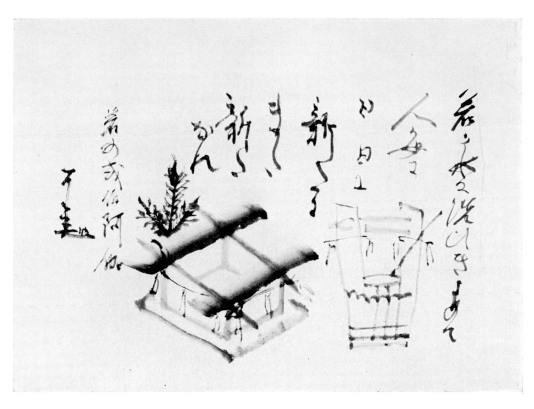

若か水に洗ひきよめて人毎に
日日に新たにまた新たなれ
若水或作阿伽　　厓

103. Purification

Have [your souls] washed in this fresh water
[of the New Year],
Have them refreshed day after day
Freshly afresh each day.

169

志ら鷺ハ有りやなしやと見へ分かぬ
雪にからすの色は津流かな　　　厓

104. Ravens

A white heron on snow is hard to distinguish;
But the ravens,
How they stand out.

An old couplet reads:

The heron standing on the snow,
　　they are not the same;
The bright moon on the flowering reeds,
　　they do not look alike.

These lines are quoted generally by Buddhists to symbolize the doctrine of identity and difference. Some of us have the fondness of reducing everything to the category of identity, oneness, or sameness. But Sengai tries strongly to bring out the aspect of the difference in contrast to the sameness, the truth often forgotten even by some Zennists.

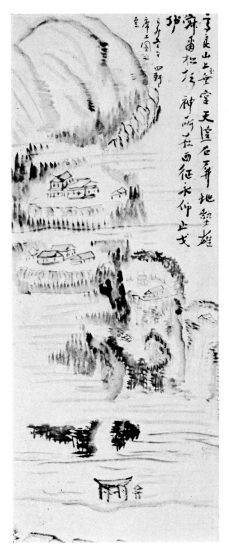

105. An Aerial View of Kōrasan

On Mt. Kōra stands the Tamadare Shintō
    Shrine
Screened by the rocks.
And the views below are sublime;
Pines and cryptomarias thickly growing,
A fit abode of the gods
Because of whose majestic powers it is that
    peace prevail in the west.

Sketched by Gai at the party held at
Shiken one winter day in the Year of
the Hare.

高良山上玉垂宮
天遶石屏地勢雄
寂爾松杉神所在
西征永仰止戈功
　　巳卯冬日四軒席
　　上図之　　厓

七福神　　厓仕合受合

106. Shintō Gateway

The Seven Gods of Fortune
[Signed] Gai
Happiness guaranteed

The three characters read: Seven gods of Fortune. These gods are Indian, Chinese and Japanese in origin. The remarkable thing is that they are all brought together over or under one Shintō gateway.

172

世の卯そと己のか誠おかへてやれ
祈らすとても神や守らむ

107. The Bullfinch (*Uso*)

Let the world's *uso* (lie) be exchanged for your *makoto* (truth); then,
whether you pray or not to the god, he will look after you.

Each year at midnight on the seventh day of the first month, a festival known
as the *Uso-gae* or Bullfinch-exchange takes place at Temman-gū Shintō Shrine in
the city of Fukuoka. On this occasion, the shrine-keepers issue little wooden
figures of the bird of passage, and the worshippers come with their old models
kept since the preceding year to have them exchanged for fresh ones. There is one
among the newly issued figurines that is golden coloured, and the person who
happens to get it is supposed to be assured of good luck in the coming year. This
shrine is dedicated to the spirit of Sugawara Michizane, of whom Sengai has also
treated in his drawings (No. 84).

Uso in Japanese has, however, another meaning; that is, a lie. Sengai here
advises the Shintō worshippers to barter the lies of the world with the *makoto* in
their hearts. *Makoto* means truth, faithfulness, or sincerity. When truths are thus
exchanged with lies, the god will surely take care of things, whether he is prayed
to or not.

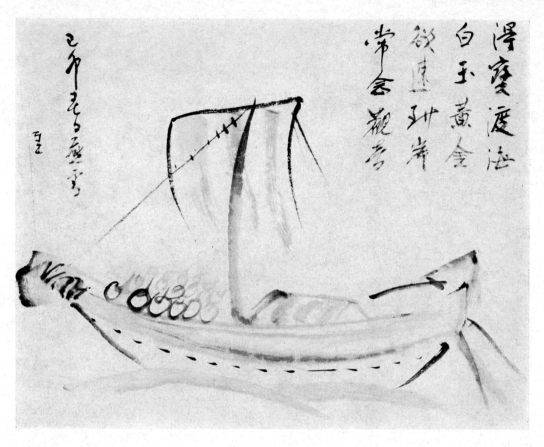

得寶渡海　白玉黄金
欲速到岸　常念観音
　　己卯春日應需　厓

108. The Treasure Ship

The ship with treasures is crossing the sea,
With white pearls and yellow gold.
If they wish a speedy and safe arrival,
Have them pray to the Kwannon all the way.

In Japan as well as in China the coming of the New Year is an auspicious occasion, and the people celebrate it by various means. The arrival at port of the Treasure Boat loaded with all kinds of treasures is one of such symbols of luck. To carry out this mission successfully the sailors are to be earnest devotees of the *Kwannon Sūtra*, the reciting of which will assure them of the accomplishment of their prayers.

There are 360 days in a year and I am master
of them [like the ancient master who said,]
'I use the twelve hours of the day [which is]
a human [institution].'

The meaning is: I am not a slave of time as time is
but the human way of trying to interpret life.

Time as we inwardly live it is no time, it cannot
be cut to pieces as minutes, hours, days and so on.
If we do, time turns into a corpse. To explain this
in Western terminology, the instant is eternity; or,
creation is a continuous one. The famous saying of
Jōshū (Chao-chou) is: 'People of the world are en-
slaved by time, but I am its master.'

一年三百六十日使得人間十二時

古池や
芭蕉飛こむ
水の音　厓

古池や
何やらぽんと
飛ひこんた　厓

池阿らは
飛て芭蕉に
聞かせたい　厓

110. Bashō and the Frog

(1)   An old pond:
Bashō jumps in,
The sound of the water!

(2)   An old pond:
Something has jumped in,
Plop!

(3)   If there were a pond around here
I would jump in
And let him hear the splash!

Sengai's fascination for Bashō's haiku on the frog is evident here. The three variations are based on Bashō's original:

An old pond,
A frog jumps in,
The sound of the water!

Some may wonder what is so extraordinary about a simple description of fact, why a frog's leap and the sound of water should be so eventful as to cause a furore. If I may say so, to Bashō's ear the frog's jumping into the old pond and the 'plop!' it produced were equalled to God's utterance, 'Let there be light!' Is this not an event of the highest order? At that instant, Bashō's mind penetrated into the secrets of creation and captured the whole universe from the beginningless beginning to the endless end. It was no mean feat.

It is the poet who transforms the everyday life of prosaic-minded people into something unique. It is the poet who sees poetry in what, to the ordinary senses, is without poetry.

Sengai's haiku too are not to be understood as mere parodies; they are in truth comments from his Zen viewpoint. For instance, he is substituting Bashō for the frog who jumps into the pond, perhaps trying to re-enact the event for the reader's inner experience.

堪　忍
気に入らぬ風も阿ろふに柳哉　　　厓

111. The Willow Tree

Patience — Winds there may be
That do not please,
But the willow!

112. A Solitary Life

A simple life in a humble hut is that
    of an unworldly one,
A bowl of rice, a cup of tea.
So absorbed in meditation,
How is he to find time for planting
    peaches and apricots?
[No matter,] the flowers in the neighbour's yard
Will blossom just the same.

活計洒然道者家　一盂午飯一盂茶
工夫豈有栽桃李　春到不妨隣院華
　　　　　　　　扶桑最初禪窟　匡

179

を月様幾つ　十三七ツ

113. Hotei

How old are you, dear moon?
Thirteen-seven?[1]

The song goes on: 'You are still young, are you not? [When you have babies] one comes, then another, and another. Who shall be held on your lap?'

The words have no positive meaning; it is just a melody soothing the baby to sleep. How whole-heartedly Hotei sings, accompanied by his little friend! He is a sort of patron saint of all young ones. Wherever he goes he is surrounded by them. His heart is so much with them that he is indeed one of the children. He is innocence itself, a veritable image of egolessness, of freedom and of humour.

Otsuki san is an endearing way of addressing the moon. To the children she is not a far-away unknown object to be explored and exploited. She is a mysterious yet an intimate being who seems always to follow us and comfort us with her soft, warm glow.

Hotei (Pu-tai) is a historical figure who is recorded as having died in A.D. 916. His biography appears in the Zen history called the *Dentōroku* (*Ch'uan-têng Lu*, or *Transmission of the Lamp*, fas. 27). But to most of us today he is always pictured as carrying a huge bag — a sort of cornucopia and a bottomless source of benevolence. He is a god of fortune ready to hand out the treasures in his bag, though he himself is a poor and unassuming soul. He incorporates the Bodhisattva Maitreya who awaits at present at the Palace of Tushita Heaven ready to appear among us when the present kalpa comes to an end.

[1] Thirteen-seven, that is, twenty.

無　事　厓

114. *Buji*

The two Chinese characters read *buji* in Japanese or *wu-shih* in Chinese. A tentative modern rendering is, free from anxiety or fear. Literally, they mean no business, no work, no event, or, all is well.

Zen master Rinzai (Lin-chi, d. 866) has this to say: 'The true aristocrat is the one who is *buji* [free from anxiety].' Aristocracy here refers to spiritual aristocracy, and not to any social distinction.

Master Tokusan (Tê-shan, 782–865) is more explicit in defining *buji*. He identifies it with *mushin*, no-mindedness: 'No mind in work, no work in mind' (*Wu shih yü hsin, wu hsin yü shih*). This epigram may be paraphrased as, 'When you are at work, have no thought of the self. Apply yourself to the work whole-heartedly. Have no other thoughts than the work on hand at the moment. Let the work, so to speak, do its own work, as if possessed by the devil, or better, by Amida Buddha. When not at work, rest. The idea of work should not pursue you; do not allow yourself to be possessed by work. Be master of your work and of yourself.'

The word master here may suggest the presence of the self or ego behind it. This is, however, not to be interpreted relatively, but absolutely. It is the master who has no equals, no superiors, as he is all by himself and in himself. He is the master that Rinzai had in mind when he said, 'Be the master wherever you may be, and your standing will always be true.' The utterance, 'Let Thy will be done' is excellent in describing the life of *buji*. Yet, strictly speaking, there is still the consciousness of God in this statement. It is best not to have even the thought of God left, however almighty he be. The Zen teacher would sometimes instruct you, 'Be like a piece of wood or stone.' This instruction is liable to be mis-interpreted as it stands, so I add: 'Be like a piece of wood or stone with human consciousness.' This consciousness, moreover, is not our ordinary consciousness; it is that which is unconsciously conscious or consciously unconscious.

Another Chinese master, Banzan Hōjaku (P'an-shan Pao-chi, d. 788), illustrates *buji* in action: 'It is like swinging the sword in the air — one does not mind whether it hits the mark or not.' Ummon Bun-en (Yün-mên Wên-yen, 864–949) is more positive: 'When the great act presents itself, it knows no rules.' 'The great act' is 'Thy will' and 'Thy will' is my 'unconscious consciousness'. This is Sengai's *buji*.

Eimyō Enju (Yung-ming Chih-chiao, 904–75), author of *Sugyō-roku* (*Tsung Ching Lu*, 'Records of the Mirror of Zen') in one hundred fascicles, has this verse:

> If you wish to know the essence of my teaching,
> Observe the lake outside the monastery gate:
> When the sun shines, how brightly it is reflected there!
> When the wind rises, how the waves surge!

Buji is often mistaken for doing nothing or idleness. Hence these wordy demonstrations.

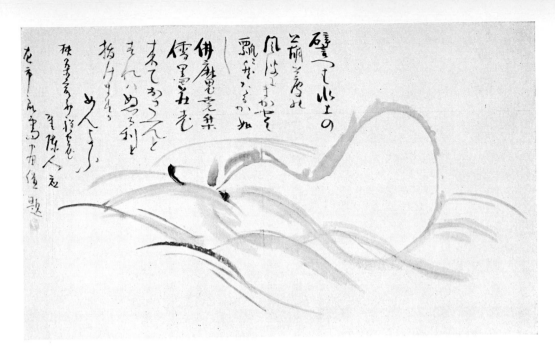

譬へは水上の葫蘆の風波にまかせて
瓢々然たるか如し
佛魔堯桀儒墨荘老来ておさへんとすれは
ぬる利と抜けますか　めんよふ

　　　　扶桑最初禅窟　厓陳人應
　　　　左市良需画住題

115. The Floating Gourd

It is like a gourd floating on the waters : it is never steady, now sinking, now rising, at the mercy of the winds. The gourd itself is altogether unconcerned. Buddha or Devil, Yao or Shun, Confucius or Mo-tzu, Lao-tzu or Chuang-tzu may all come to take hold of it. But the gourd will elusively slip out of their grasp. Amazing !

Pictured and inscribed by Gai the Useless, in response to the request of Saichiro.

The ultimate reality or the Tao (Way) is absolutely independent of all our efforts to comprehend it. When we think we have it at last, it steps out of our grasp. Yet it is floating before our eyes regardless of our intellectual attempts to nail it down to a fixed board of comprehensibility. As long as it is looked upon dichotomously as an object, it is always out of our reach. The point is therefore to identify ourselves with it and leave ourselves to float with it on the ever-flowing stream of life.

道難救周　德不化胡
叱　青牛迷途
　　文化丁丑夏
　　　扶桑最初禪窟　厓陳人

116. Lao-tzu

His Way (*tao*) failed to save Chou from decline
His Virtue (*tê*) did not convert the barbarians —
Pshaw!
The darkish ox knows not which way to turn now!

Lao-tzu (fifth century B.C.) wrote a book known as the *Tao-tê Ching. Tao* is Way, *tê*, Virtue, and *Ching*, a canonical book. But Lao-tzu, with all his wisdom and virtue, could not save the Chou dynasty from its downfall. Moreover, he is legendarily considered to be an incarnate Buddha or one of Buddha's chief disciples, originally from India, where he supposedly failed to convert the Hindus to Buddhism. Having been useless in the two characteristics by which he is best known, Lao-tzu finds his favourite animal now at a loss where to go. This is not meant by Sengai to be a criticism of Lao-tzu's philosophy. He is rather lamenting over the worldly way of most of us.

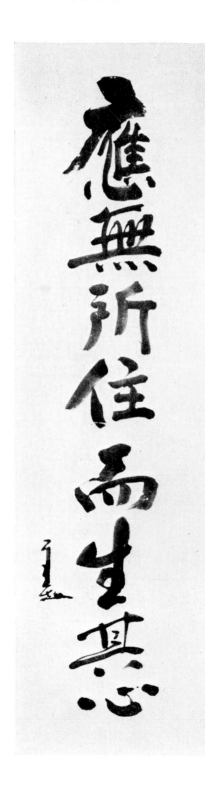

Cherish a thought which does not attach itself
to anything.
[Or, Cherish no thoughts that have an abode.]

This is quoted from the *Vajracchedikā-prajñāpāramitā-sūtra*, popularly known as the *Diamond Sūtra*. A thought that attaches itself to something is contaminated with an egoistic design and is thus impure. Thought is a general term for anything that is stirred in the mind (*citta*). A thought that has no abode is one that is awakened in the depths of that subjectivity which is Emptiness (*śūnyatā*). To use Meister Eckhart's terminology, it is a heart of *Abgeschiedenheit* (detachment). Ontologically, Emptiness is Being *per se*, and morally, it corresponds to non-attachment, or abodeless-ness, or selflessness.

應無所住而生其心　　厓

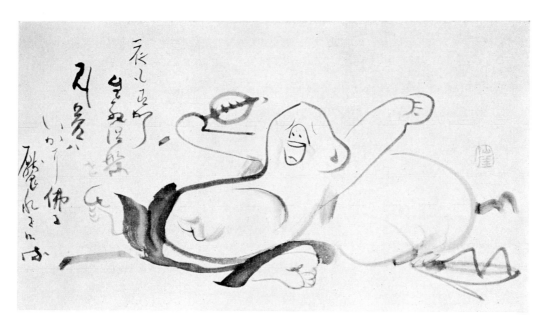

夜もすから生死涅槃を見し夢ハ
いか·に佛に驀れにけ流

118. Buddha-possessed

Throughout the night,
I have been annoyed by the thoughts of
  nirvana and samsara :
[How exhausting the dream !]
Apparently I had been made captive of Buddha.

In Zen we speak of being over-possessed by goodness or holiness. Every kind of obsession is considered undesirable. Says Master Jōshū (Chao-chou, 778–897): 'I do not like to hear the word ''Buddha''.' Sometimes he warns his disciples: 'Do not stay where Buddha is; pass on quickly where he is not.' The idea is, when you are too obsessed with the concept of Buddha, or of nirvāna, or of samsāra (birth-and-death), or of enlightenment, you are hypnotized by it and can never attain to the right understanding of it. The way to approach Buddhahood or enlightenment is to concretize the logic: A is A because A is not-A, in your own experience. This is to understand the un-understandable.

Sengai depicts himself as Hotei awaking from a long and exhausting nightmare such as is described above. Hotei is the very symbol of spiritual freedom.

187

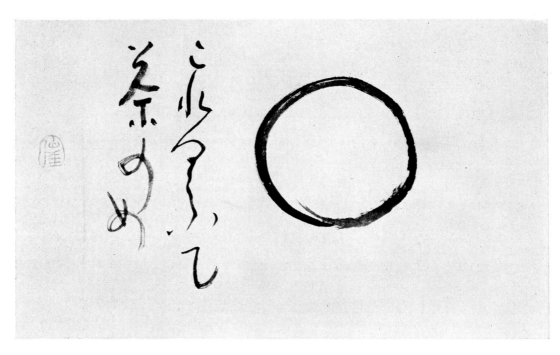

これくふて茶のめ

119. Circle

Eat this and have a cup of tea.

EXPLANATORY NOTES

by Shokin Furuta

IV.   En-mei in Japanese. En means far, Mei clear. This was probably written for the tablet to be hung in the tea-house.

IX.   Behind the Shōfukuji Temple, Hakata.

2.   Sengai drew Amida, the Buddha of Infinite Light, on the rubbed copy taken from the Sukhāvatī sūtra stone of the Munakata Grand Shrine in Fukuoka Prefecture, when he was 79 years old.

4.   By the completion of the translation of the Kegon Sūtra (Buddhavataṃsaka-nāma Mahāvaipulya Sūtra) into Chinese, the Kegon (Avatamsaka) sect was founded, and developed into the most philosophical sect in Buddhism. It was transmitted to Japan in the Nara Period.

6.   Tenbōrin means 'Revolving the wheel of Dharma' (Dharma-ćakra-pravar-tana). This was probably written for the tablet to be hung under the eaves of the Ceremony Hall.

7.   This kind of composition of Kwannon is called Ṣuigetsu-Kwannon or Water-moon Kwannon.
This composition of Kwannon is very rare, and is a kind of weeping-willow Kwannon. She holds a twig of the weeping-willow in her hand. The name comes from the belief that she complies with every prayer of all sentient beings like the weeping-willow bends before the wind.

10.   Bon is the abbreviation of Gibon, Sengai's given name.

12.1.   A. wise and virtuous emperor who ruled the Chou state around 1100 B.C with his system of Li-Yue.

2.   Tara is the abbreviation of the Tara-kankan which means to read Sūtras only and with a narrow view.

18.   The incarnation of the star of the South Pole. Believed to have lived around the eleventh century.

28.   By the traditional Japanese Zen way, Hyakujō reads Hajo.

35.   Rakuyo (Lo-Yang) was the capital.

39.   A Japanese wine.

40. Za means sitting; Zen, meditation.

47. There is an old saying: 'Add the bamboo to the drawing of the tiger to prove that it is not the cat.' The drawing of the tiger is often associated with the bamboo.

48. There is no connection in thought between these two scrolls, but they were mounted as a pair.

52. The original text says Naniwa-zu. Zu is the sonant of Tsu which means a landing place or a wharf. It is an associate word to Yo-o-wataru which means 'steer one's way in the voyage of life'.

60. Mt. Fuji, a dormant volcano, has been worshipped by Japanese as a Holy mountain of the guardian god. In the *Taketori Monogatari*, it is said that on the top of Mt. Fuji the royal elixir of immortality which the Princess Kaguya left behind was burnt, the smoke from which would coil up forever.

Fuji can be written in two ways in Sino-Japanese characters, one which means 'not-two' and the other which means 'wealthy gentleman'. 'Not-two' means non-dual and in the Buddhist position of non-dualism, Buddhists, especially devotees of Zen, often use this expression.

62. Also known as Zenne Daishi. He is recorded in the *Transmission of the Lamp*, fas. 27.

73. In Hakata, Fukuoka Prefecture.

85. Mt. Rai, in Itoshima county, Fukuoka Prefecture.

92. 'Long face' implies contempt or disdain.

94. A Zen master of the T'ang dynasty. He is said to have always fished for shrimps and eaten them. He pretended to be a mad monk and is recorded in the *Transmission of the Lamp*.

96. Outskirts of Hakata, Fukuoka Prefecture.

97. The Western Capital means Dazai-fu, in Kyūshū. In 664, Dazai-fu was founded as the centre of local government. It is well known for its relics of the ancient civilization.

102. Dainichi in Japanese, Mahāvairocana in Sanskrit.

103. Wakamizu in Japanese. The original text says 'made of Waka (fresh) or Aka (water, Argha in Sanskrit)'. Argha means pure water. It is possible that the Japanese pronunciation Waka comes from Aka, the Japanese pronunciation of Argha.

105. Mt. Kora. South of Kurume City, Fukuoka Prefecture.
Taguchi Shiken, a poet and a friend of Sengai, lived in Hakata.

108. The scroll of the treasure ship is often hung up at the New Year as an auspicious token.

The *Kwannon Sūtra* is a chapter of the *Lotus Sūtra*.

113. It may refer to the seventh hour of the thirteenth day of the moon. Two nights before the full moon, the moon is still young. The seventh hour is too early in the evening for the moon to rise high above the horizon. Hence, 'you are (too) young'.

117. Kongō-kyō in Japanese.